Baltimore in Bloom

Pam Bono Designs, Inc.

1

Baltimore in Bloom

©2002 Pam Bono Designs, Inc., publisher.

ISBN 0-9661500-2-3
Manufactured in the
United States Of America
First Printing

We make every effort to insure that the contents of the book are correct and understandable.

Editor-In-Chief: Pam Bono
Editorial Assistant: Gigi Thompson
Editors: Gigi Thompson, Patricia Nicolas and Robert Bono
Art Director and Book Design: Pam Bono
Technical Editors: Pam Bono, Robert Bono, and Gigi Thompson
Graphic Illustrations: Pam Bono
Photographer: Christopher Marona
Photo Stylists: Christopher Marona, Pam Bono, Robert Bono and Gigi Thompson.
Marketing & Distribution Director: Pam Bono Designs, Inc.

Where to write to us:
Pam Bono Designs, Inc.
P.O. Box 1049
Durango, CO 81302

Web site:
http://www.pambonodesigns.com

Baltimore In Bloom embroidery collection is available at participating Husqvarna Viking Sewing Machine and Pfaff Sewing Machine Dealers. It is a multi-format CD with the following formats: V.I.P, HUS, SHV, PCS, PES, CSD, SEW, XXX, and DST.

*Some products mentioned in this book may be trademarked, but not to be acknowledged as so.

Dedication:

This book is dedicated to two people who play an important role in our personal and professional lives:

To my friend, Pat Nicolas who owns Animas Quilts, "The Best Of The West!" There was a big gap. It took a very special person to fill it. Thanks for being there for the best and the worst. I appreciate our friendship.

Pam

To our photographer and friend, Chris Marona: This book is the culmination of perfect teamwork. Without you, your wonderful sense of humor, and your tremendous talent, this book would not be what it is. We are so proud of your work, and "you sure know where to move those lights"!

Pam and Robert

Quilt Designs by Pam & Robert Bono.

Embroidery Designs by
Pam & Robert Bono.

Quilting by Faye Gooden

Digitizing by Barbara Kissinger

Finishing by Suzanne Gamble, Bonnie
Colonna, and Gigi Thompson.

Photography by Christopher Marona

We have a great friend. Her name is Wanda Nelson. Wanda is an avid quilter who is now retired and owned a fabulous quilt shop in Farmington, New Mexico.. Our special thanks to Wanda for driving 45 miles to cook us surprise lunches so that we didn't have to stop working. Not only is she a true friend, but one of the few people we have ever known who has conquered great tragedies with even greater strength.

We love you Wanda!

Special Thanks to:

Gigi Thompson, our personal assistant, for her relentless efforts to make certain that everything is beautiful and correct. Thanks for work above and beyond the call of duty. It's a pleasure to have you with us.

Theresa Robinson of Viking Sewing Machine Company for recognizing the potential, and being such a joy to work with.

Sandy Medearis, the Manager of the General Palmer House Hotel in Durango, Colorado. It was such a joy to do location shots in the hotel that you so artfully decorated. We appreciate your hospitality very much.

Britt and Paul Toppenberg for allowing us to photograph in your lovely home.

Pat and Tammy Nicolas for allowing us to do our final location photography in your shop, and for your help and thoughtfullness.

To Faye Gooden, whom in our opinion has become the quilting guru! Your work has become art. Thanks for a great job.

Our friend and Viking educator, Bonnie Colonna for executing the lovely violet embroidery projects, and creating the Rose Of Sharon vest. Your help and talent is greatly appreciated.

Our friend Suzanne Gamble, owner of the Durango Design Center. Thanks for your friendship and beautiful finishing.

Husqvarna Viking Sewing Machine Company for the loan of our Designer 1 machines that made it possible to sew such beautiful embroideries.

RJR Fabrics for your supply of wonderful fabrics, and for getting us the sample cuts needed on time.

P & B Textiles for supplying us with your lovely line to use in this book. It is greatly appreciated.

Robison Anton Textile Company for supplying us with the beautiful array of rayon thread for all of the embroideries.

Mr. Jan Carr of Clover Needlecraft for supplying your Bias Makers and press on bias tape.

Quilts pieced by: Pam Bono, Robert Bono, Gigi Thompson and Patty Brost.

Jacqui Dacko, my teacher, and a talented young graphic artist, who led me through the learning curve of a new computer program. Thanks for your patience!

Introduction:

It seems as though every time Robert and I do a new book, we are given the incredible opportunity of working with very talented people in a new and exciting field. We are also given the chance to learn something that we have never experienced before.

This book is about quilts. It's about making them, embellishing them, and using them to the best of your advantage to enhance or change the surroundings in which they are placed. It is jam packed full of accessory projects that will delight your friends and family as tokens of your caring.

Designing and learning about machine embroideries opened up an entirely new aspect of what can be accomplished with a little creativity, and a desire to make a quilting project even more attractive and eye catching.

In making the designs, you are the artist. You may choose your own color schemes to fit into the decor that is part of your personality. You may add lovely embroideries or quilting designs that are your favorites. We are giving you the empty canvas, and encouraging you to paint it with the fabric and tread of your choice.

Baltimore In Bloom has been created with a great deal of joy, excitement, and enthusiasm on our part. Our fondest desire is that you, the quilter may enjoy its contents as much as we have enjoyed putting it together for you.

Quilting Is A Gift Of Creativity & Joy!

Pam and Robert Bono

4

Table of Contents

Rose Of Sharon

Baltimore Violet
Tablecloth &
Kitchen
Accessories.
Pages 46-49

Baltimore Roses
Quilt and
Accessories.
Pages 68-76

Pineapple Welcome
Sign, Table Runner,
and Place Mats
Pages 77-82

Cotton Puffs
Quilt and
Accessories
Pages 50-56

Grapes On The Vine
Tablecloths and
Accessories
Pages 57-62

Water Lily Quilt
& Accessories.
Pages 83-89

Vase Of Flowers
Buffet Cloth and
Place Mats
Pages 90-96

Fleur-de-Lis
Shower Curtain
Pages 63-67

Embroidered
Throw
Pages 97-100

Learning Our Techniques

**The techniques that are shown on the following pages are used throughout projects in the book. Please refer to these techniques frequently, and practice them with scraps.

STRIP PIECING

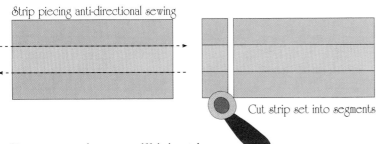

Strip piecing anti-directional sewing

Cut strip set into segments

For some projects, you'll join strips of different fabrics to make what is called a strip set. Project directions not only show illustrations of each strip set, but specify how many strip sets to make, how many segments are to be cut from each strip set, and the specific size of each strip and segment. To sew a strip set, match each pair of strips with right sides facing. Stitch through both layers along one long edge. When sewing multiple strips in a set, practice "anti-directional" stitching to keep strips straight. As you add strips, sew each new seam in the *opposite direction* from the last one. This distributes tension evenly in both directions, and keeps your strip set from getting warped and wobbly.

DIAGONAL CORNERS

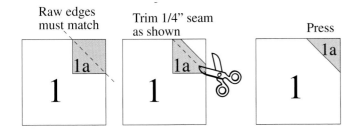

Raw edges must match   Trim 1/4" seam as shown   Press

This technique turns squares into sewn triangles. It is especially helpful if the corner triangle is very small, because it's easier to cut and handle a square than a small triangle. By sewing squares to squares, you don't have to guess where the seam allowance meets, which can be difficult with triangles. Project instructions give the size of the fabric pieces needed. These sizes given in the cutting instructions *include* seam allowance. The base triangle is either a square or rectangle, but the contrasting corner is *always* a square.

1. To make a diagonal corner, with right sides facing, match the small square to one corner of the base fabric. It is important that raw edges match perfectly and do not shift during sewing.

2. As a seam guide, you may wish to draw or press a diagonal line from corner to corner. For a quick solution to this

time consuming technique, refer to our instructions on the following pages for The Angler 2.

3. Stitch the small square diagonally from corner to corner. Trim seam allowance as shown on the diagonal corner square only, leaving the base fabric untrimmed for stability and keeping the corner square. Press the diagonal corner square over as shown.

4. Many units in the projects have multiple diagonal corners or ends. When these are the same size, and cut from the same fabric, the identifying unit letter is the same. But, if the unit has multiple diagonal pieces that are different in size and/or color, the unit letters are different. These pieces are joined to the main unit in alphabetical order.

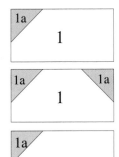

5. Many of our projects utilize diagonal corners on diagonal corners as shown below. In this case, diagonal corners are added in alphabetical order once again. First join diagonal corner, trim and press out; then add the second diagonal corner, trim and press out as shown.

6. Our designs also utilize diagonal corners on joined units

Diagonal corners on diagonal Corners - Join corners in alphabetical order.

such as strip sets. In this case, the joined units will have one unit number in the center of the unit as shown at right, with the diagonal corner having its own unit number.

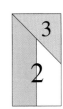

Diagonal Corner on combined, joined units.

Diagonal Ends

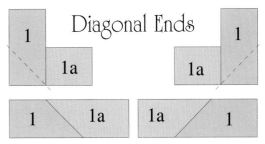

Diagonal End - Left Slant   Diagonal End - Right Slant

1. This method joins two rectangles on the diagonal and eliminates the difficulty of measuring and cutting a trapezoid. It is similar to the diagonal corner technique, but here you work with two rectangles. Our project instructions specify the size of each rectangle.

2. To sew diagonal ends, place rectangles perpendicular to each other with right sides facing, matching corners to be sewn.

3. Before you sew, mark or press the diagonal stitching line, and check the right side to see if the line is angled in the desired direction.

4. Position the rectangles under the needle, leading with the top edge. Sew a diagonal seam to the opposite edge.

5. Check the right side to see that the seam is angled correctly. Then press the seam and trim excess fabric from the seam allowance.

6. As noted in Step 2, the direction of the seam makes a difference. Make mirror-image units with this in mind, or you can put different ends on the same strip. This technique is wonderful for making *continuous* binding strips. Please note on illustration below, diagonal ends are made first; then diagonal corners may be added in alphabetical order.

7. Refer to Step 6 in *diagonal corner section*. Diagonal ends may be added to joined units in the same manner as shown below.

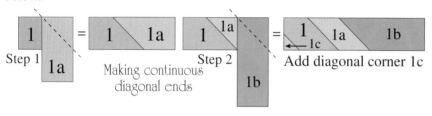

Making continuous diagonal ends

Add diagonal corner 1c

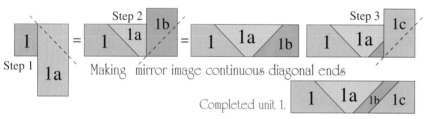

Making mirror image continuous diagonal ends

Completed unit 1.

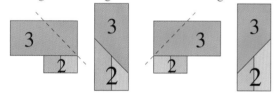

Making mirror image combined unit diagonal ends.

HALF SQUARE TRIANGLES

1. Many patchwork designs are made by joining two contrasting triangles to make a square. Many people use the grid method when dozens of triangles are required in a design. For the designs in this book, however we use a simple way to make one or more half square triangles. To do so draw or press a diagonal line from corner to corner on the back of the lightest colored square.

2. As an extra tip, we have found that spraying the fabric with spray starch before cutting the squares to be used keeps them from distorting. A bit more fabric may be used, however it is a quick and easy technique.

3. Place squares right sides together and stitch on the line. Trim the seam as shown and press.

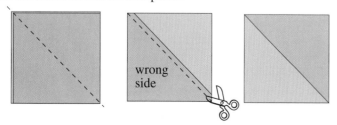

wrong side

4. The illustration at right shows how half square triangle units are marked in the book. A diagonal line is always shown, separating the two fabric colors. The unit number is always shown in the center of the square.

MACHINE PIECING

An accurate, consistant 1/4" seam allowance is essential for good piecing. If each seam varies by the tiniest bit, the difference multiplies greatly by the time the block is completed. Before you start a project, be sure your machine is in good working order and that you can sew a precise 1/4" seam allowance. Refer to instructions and illustrations for use of The Angler 2 in this section to aid with accurate seams.

1. Set your sewing machine to 12-14 stitches per inch. Use 100%-cotton or cotton/polyester sewing thread.

2. Match pieces to be sewn with right sides facing. Sew each seam from cut edge to cut edge of the fabric piece. It is not necessary to backstitch, because most seams will be crossed and held by another seam.

SEWING AN "X"

1. When triangles are pieced with other units, seams should cross in an "X" on the back. If the joining seam goes precisely through the center of the "X", the triangle will have a nice sharp point on the front.

PRESS AND PIN

1. To make neat corners and points, seams must meet precisely. Pressing and pinning can help achieve matched seams.

2. To press, set your iron on cotton. Use an up-and-down motion, lifting the iron from spot to spot. Sliding the iron back and forth can push seams out of shape. First press the seam flat on the wrong side; then open the piece and press the right side.

3. Press patchwork seam allowance to one side, not open as in dressmaking. If possible, press toward the darker fabric to avoid seam allowance showing through light fabric. Press seam allowances in opposite directions from row to row. By offsetting seam allowances at each intersection, you reduce the bulk under the patchwork. This is more important than pressing seam allowances toward dark fabric.

4. Use pins to match seam lines. With right sides facing, align opposing seams, nesting seam allowances. On the top piece, push a pin through the seam line 1/4" from the edge. Then push the pin through the bottom seam and set it. Pin all matching seams; then stitch the joining seams, removing pins as you sew.

EASING FULLNESS

1. Sometimes two units that should be the same size are slightly different. When joining such units, pin-match opposing seams. Sew the seam with the shorter piece on top. As you sew, the feed dogs ease the fullness on the bottom piece. This is called "sewing with a baggy bottom."

2. If units are too dissimilar to ease without puckering, check each one to see if the pieces were correctly cut and that the seams are 1/4" wide. Remake the unit that varies the most from the desired size.

CHAIN PIECING

1. Chain piecing is an efficient way to sew many units in one operation, saving time and thread. Line up several units to be sewn. Sew the first unit as usual, but at the end of the seam do not backstitch, clip the thread, or lift the presser foot. Instead, feed the next unit right on the heels of the first. There will be a little twist of thread between each unit. Sew as many seams as you like on a chain. Keep the chain intact to carry to the ironing board and clip the threads as you press.

> If you are a beginner, or if you are not familiar with our quick piecing techniques, please read about the techniques and practice them before you begin any of the projects in the book!

MAKING STRAIGHT-GRAIN FRENCH-FOLD BINDING.

1. Each project specifies the number of cross grain strips to cut for binding. To join strips , match the ends perpendicular as for diagonal ends. Join strips end to end in this manner to make one continuous strip that is the length specified in our project instructions.

2. These instructions are for French-fold, straight-grain binding. Double binding is stronger than one layer so it better protects the edges, where a quilt suffers the most wear. We like French-fold binding because it is easier to make than bias binding, and requires less fabric.

3. After joining strips, press the binding in half, along the length of the strip, wrong sides together.

4. Follow the illustrations and begin by positioning the binding on the front of the quilt top, in the center of any side. Leave a 3" tail of binding free before the point where you begin to sew.

5. Stitch through all layers using 1/4" seam. Stop stitching 1/4" from the quilt corner and backstitch. (Placing a pin at the 1/4" point beforehand will show you where to stop.) Remove the quilt from the machine.

6. Rotate the quilt a quarter turn. Fold the binding straight up, away from the corner, and make a 45° angle fold.

7. Bring the binding straight down in line with the next edge, leaving the top fold even with the raw edge of the previously sewn side. Begin stitching at the top edge, sewing through all layers, and reinforcing top edge. Stitch all corners in this manner.

8. Stop stitching as you approach the beginning point. Fold the 3" tail of binding over itself and pin. The end of the binding will overlap this folded section. Continue stitching through all layers to 1" beyond the folded tail. Trim away any extra binding.

9. Trim the batting and backing nearly even with the seam allowance, leaving a little extra to fill out the binding.

10. Fold the binding over the seam allowance to the back. When turned, the beginning fold conceals the raw end of the binding.

11. Blind stitch the folded edge of the binding to the backing fabric. Fold and miter into the binding at back corners.

STRAIGHT-GRAIN FRENCH-FOLD BINDING.

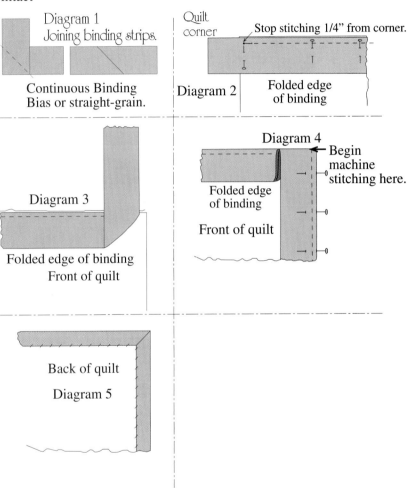

Diagram 1
Joining binding strips.
Continuous Binding
Bias or straight-grain.

Quilt corner — Stop stitching 1/4" from corner.
Diagram 2   Folded edge of binding

Diagram 3
Folded edge of binding
Front of quilt

Diagram 4   Begin machine stitching here.
Folded edge of binding
Front of quilt

Back of quilt
Diagram 5

The Angler 2 ™

Robert invented the first Angler between our first and second books for Oxmoor House. He watched me drawing diagonal line seam guides that took forever! I recall him saying "There has got to be a quicker way!" He found a quicker way. This little tool is now used by millions of quilter's all over the world with results that cut piecing time in half, after a bit of practice. The instructions and illustrations on the following pages are shown for the new upgrade, allowing you to make up to 7 3/4 squares. It can be purchased where ever sewing notions are sold.

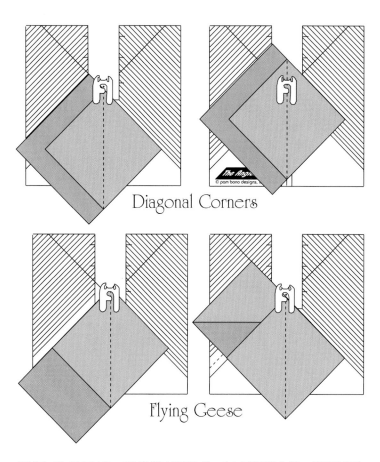

Diagonal Corners

Flying Geese

DIAGONAL CORNERS & FLYING GEESE

1. Align diagonal corners with raw edges matching. Line fabric up so that right side of square is aligned with first 45° line on right as shown above, with the tip of the fabric under the needle. No seam guide lines will need to be drawn unless the square is larger than 7 3/4". As feed dogs pull the fabric through the machine, keep fabric aligned with the diagonal lines on the right until center line of The Angler 2 bottom is visible.

2. Keep the tip of the square on this line as the diagonal corner is fed through the machine. Trim seam as shown in our "quick piecing" technique section and press.

3. For Flying Geese, sew first diagonal corner. Trim seam for diagonal corner and press; then join second diagonal corner. Trim seam and press. Overlap will give you accurate 1/4" seam allowance.

ACCURATE 1/4" SEAMS

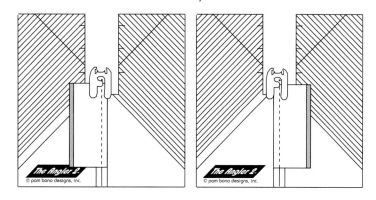

1. Referring to illustration of 1/4" seam line, note that fabric is lined up on 1/4" seam line on The Angler 2, and that stitching is along center guide line. To take a full 1/4" seam, line fabric up on 1/4" seam line as shown. If you want a "scant" 1/4" seam, line fabric up so that the seam guide line shows.

2. Please note that we recommend a "scant" 1/4" seam because your seams are more accurately 1/4" when they are pressed.

DIAGONAL ENDS

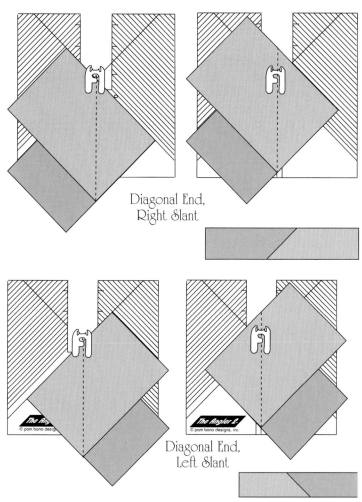

Diagonal End, Right Slant

Diagonal End, Left Slant

1. For both slants, prepare rectangles with raw edges matching. For right slant, align top rectangle with the first 45° line on right side of The Angler 2.

2. Bottom rectangle should align on first 45° left line as shown. As feed dogs pull fabric through machine, keep fabric aligned with the diagonal lines on the right until center line on The Angler 2 bottom is visible. Keep the top of the rectangle on this line as it is fed through the machine. Trim seam and press.

3. For left slant, line top rectangle up with the first 45° line on left side of The Angler 2 as shown. As rectangles are fed through the machine, keep top rectangle aligned with left diagonal lines on The Angler 2. This technique is great for joining binding strips.

Using Our Instructions....

The following points explain how the instructions in our book are organized. You will find that all projects are made easier if you read this section thoroughly and follow each tip.

• Yardages are based on 44-45" wide fabric, allowing for up to 4% shrinkage. 100% cotton fabric is recommended for the quilt top and backing. Wash, dry and press fabrics before cutting.

• At the beginning of each project, we tell you which techniques are used so you can practice them before beginning. Seam allowances *are included* in all stated measurements and cutting.

• The materials list provides you with yardage requirements for the project. We have included the exact number of inches needed to make the project, with yardages given to the nearest 1/8 yard. By doing this, we are giving you the option to purchase extra yardage if you feel you may need more.

• A color key accompanies each materials list, matching each fabric with the color-coded illustrations given with the project directions. We have made an effort to match the colors in the graphics to the actual fabric colors used in the project.

• Cutting instructions are given for each fabric, the first cut, indicated by a •, is usually a specific number of cross grain strips. The second cut, indicated by *, specifies how to cut those strips into smaller pieces, or "segments." The identification of each piece follows in parenthesis, consisting of the block letter and unit number that corresponds to the assembly diagram. For pieces used in more than one unit, several unit numbers are given.

• Organize all cut pieces in zip top bags, and label each bag with the appropriate unit numbers. We use masking tape on the bags to label them. We can not emphasize the importance of this enough as it avoids confusion and keeps the pieces stored safely until they are needed. Arrange all fabric colors, in their individual bags with like fabrics together, making it easy to find a specific unit and fabric color.

• In order to conserve fabric, we have carefully calculated the number of units that can be cut from specified strips. In doing this, units may be cut in two or three different places in the cutting instructions, from a variety of strips. So that cut units may be organized efficiently, the units that appear in more than one strip are shown in red on the cutting list. This immediately tells you that there will be more of that specific unit. Additional cuts are not only shown in red, but the words "add to" are shown within the parenthesis so you may keep that zip top bag open, knowing in advance there will be more units to add.

• Large pieces such as sashing and borders are generally cut first to assure you have enough fabric. To reduce further waste of fabric, you may be instructed to cut some pieces from a first-cut strip, and then cut that strip down to a narrower width to cut additional pieces.

• Cutting instructions are given for the entire quilt as shown. To make one block, see information under "Making One Block."

• Cutting and piecing instructions are given in a logical step-by-step progression. Follow this order always to avoid having to rip out in some cases. Although there are many assembly graphics, we strongly suggest reading the written instructions along with looking at the graphics. Some blocks are further divided into sections, which are joined together according to written instructions.

• Every project has one or more block designs. Instructions include block illustrations that show the fabric color, and the numbered units.

• Individual units are assembled first. Use one or more of the "quick piecing" techniques described on pages 7-9.

• Strip set illustrations show the size of the segments to be cut from that strip set. The illustration also designates how many strip sets are to be made, and the size of the strips. The strip set segments are then labeled as units within the block illustration. Keep strip set segments in their own labeled zip top bag.

• Each unit in the assembly diagram is numbered. The main part of the unit is indicated with a number only. A diagonal line represents a seam where a diagonal corner or end is attached. Each diagonal piece is numbered with the main unit number plus a letter (example: 1a).

• Many extra illustrations are given throughout the projects for assembly of unusual or multiple units for more clarity.

• Piecing instructions are given for making one block. Make the number of blocks stated in the project illustrations to complete the project as shown.

• For embroidery areas, larger pieces of fabric are indicated in the cutting list so that the fabric will fit in your hoop. Instructions are given for cutting the completed embroideries down to the size required to fit into the quilt or accessory design.

HOW TO MAKE ONE BLOCK

Cutting instructions are given for making the quilt as shown. But there may be times that you want to make just one block for a project of your own design. All you have to do is count, or divide if preferred.

With each cutting list there is an illustration for the blocks (s). Unit numbers in the cutting list correspond with the units in the illustration. Count how many of each unit are in the block illustration. Instead of cutting the number shown on the cutting list, cut the number you need for one block. Should you wish to make two or more blocks, multiply the number of units X the number of blocks you wish to make.

If you prefer, you can figure out just from the cutting list. If the quilt shown has 20 blocks, for example, then divide each quantity by 20 to determine how many pieces are needed for one block.

LIST OF SUGGESTED SUPPLIES TO START

1. Rotary cutter: There are several different types of rotary cutters on the market. They are available in different shapes and sizes. Choose the one that is the most comfortable in your hand. Remember, the larger the blade, the longer it will last. Also purchase replacement blades.
2. Cutting mat: The size of the mat is based of course, on the size of your cutting area. We use the 23" x 35" mat.
3. Acrylic rulers: We use several sizes. The favorites are: 8" x 24", 6" x 18", and the most used is the 3 1/2" x 12".
4. Sewing thread. Use a good quality cotton or cotton/poly thread.
5. Pins and pincushion. We especially like the long, thin, fine pins for quilting.
6. Seam ripper. We all use them frequently. We call them the "Unsewers!"
7. Scissors. Here again, we use two or three different sizes to do different jobs.
8. Iron and ironing board. We use June Tailor's pressing mats next to our sewing machines for pressing smaller pieces.
9. Zip top bags, masking tape, and of course, The Angler 2!
10. If you are going to do the embroideries, you will need good marking pens, stabilizer and a supply of machine embroidery needles, as they should be changed every 8 hours of sewing.

Baltimore Tulip

Baltimore Tulip is the perfect design to start with if you are new to piecing. Two simple "quick piecing" techniques are used here, giving results that look as though you have been quilting for years.

The cheerful embroideries are used to embellish the pieced top cloth, but can easily be substituted with simple quilting designs if an embroidery machine is still on your "wish list."

Patchwork tablecloth finishes to: 51" square.
Block A finishes to: 11" square.
Block B finishes to: 10 1/2" square.
Embroidered undercloth finishes to: 60" square.
Place Mats finish to: 14 3/4" x 18 3/4"
Napkins finish to 12" square.

MATERIALS

	Fabric I (ivory with gold check)	Need 72 3/4"	2 1/8 yards
	Fabric II (dark red print)	Need 47"	1 3/8 yards
	Fabric IIII (small gold check)	Need 10 1/2"	3/8 yard
	Fabric IV (bright red print)	Need 7 1/2"	1/4 yard
	Fabric V (light olive print)	Need 14"	1/2 yard
	Fabric VI (dark olive print)	Need 5"	1/4 yard
	Backing		3 1/4 yards

For Embroideries:

Robison Anton #40 weight rayon embroidery thread: #2493 Lt. Bronze (dk. gold), #2606 TH Gold (lt. yellow), #2418 Red Berry (bright red), #2252 Russet (dark red), #2211 Nile (lt. green), and #2738 Pro Erin (dark green).

Techniques Used: Diagonal Corners and Diagonal Ends.

Cutting instructions shown in red indicate that the quantity of units is combined and cut in 2 or more different places to conserve fabric.

CUTTING

All "Q" units in cutting instructions stand for "quilt top." These are units that are not incorporated into the specific blocks, but are on the tablecloth top.

☐ From Fabric I, cut: (ivory with gold check)

- Four 16" wide strips. From these, cut:
  * Twelve – 12" x 16" (Q1, and Q2 for 150 x 240mm hoop). When complete, center embroideries. For Q1 cut eight 8" squares, and for Q2, cut four 7 1/2" x 8" pieces. Finding the embroidery center, cut 3 3/4" from center on two opposite sides, and 4" from center on remaining two sides.
  * Four – 3 1/2" x 7 3/4" (A8)
  * Eight – 2 1/2" sq. (A1, B1)
  * Four – 2 1/2" x 6 3/4" (B8)
  * Sixteen – 2" sq. (A10a, A10b)
- One 3 3/4" wide strip. From this, cut:
  * Eight – 3 3/4" x 4 1/4" (A11, A15)
- One 3 1/2" wide strip. From this, cut:
  * Four – 3 1/2" x 4 3/4" (A7)
  * Four – 2 1/2" x 4 3/4" (B7)
- One 1 1/2" wide strip. From this, cut:
  * Sixteen – 1 1/2" sq. (A9b, B11a, B15a)

■ From Fabric II, cut: (dark red print)

- One 4 1/2" wide strip. From this, cut:
  * Eight – 1 1/2" x 4 1/2" (A5, B5)
  * Eight – 1 1/2" x 3 1/2" (A4, B4)
- Fifteen 2 1/2" wide strips. Six strips for straight-grain binding. From remaining nine strips, cut:
  * Four – 2 1/2" x 26" (Q8) Piece two together to = two 51 1/2" strips.
  * Two – 2 1/2" x 22 1/2" (Q7)
  * Eight – 2 1/2" x 13" (Q6)
  * Four – 2 1/2" x 11" (Q5)
  * Eight – 2 1/2" x 4 3/4" (B10)
  * Eight – 2 1/2" x 4 1/4" (A10)
- Four 1 1/4" wide strips. From these, cut:
  * Four – 1 1/4" x 22 1/2" (Q4)

☐ From Fabric III, cut: (small gold check)

- Four 2 5/8" wide strips. From these, cut:
  * Four – 4 3/4" x 22 1/2" (Q3)
  * Eight – 2 1/2" squares (A13, B13)

■ From Fabric IV, cut: (bright red print)

- Three 2 1/2" wide strips. From these, cut:
  * Eight – 2 1/2" x 4 3/4" (B9)
  * Eight – 2 1/2" x 4 1/4" (A9)
  * Eight – 2 1/2" sq. (A6, B6)

▨ From Fabric V, cut: (light olive print)

- One 4 3/4" wide strip. From this, cut:
  * Twelve – 2 3/4" x 4 3/4" (B11, B14, B15)
  * Eight – 1 1/2" sq. (A9a)
- Two 2 1/2" wide strips. From these, cut:
  * Four – 2 1/2" x 2 3/4" (B12)
  * Sixteen – 2 1/2" sq. (B10a, B10b)
  * Four – 2 1/4" x 2 1/2" (A12)
- One 2 1/4" wide strip. From this, cut:
  * Four – 2 1/4" x 4 1/4" (A14)
  * Twelve – 2" sq. (B9a, B9b)
- One 2" wide strip. From this, cut:
  * Four – 2" sq. (add to B9a, B9b above)
  * Eight – 1 1/4" sq. (A13a, B13a)

■ From Fabric VI, cut: (dark olive print)

- Two 1 3/4" wide strips. From these, cut:
  * Eight – 1 3/4" x 3 3/4" (A3, B3)
  * Eight – 1 3/4" x 2 1/2" (A2, B2)
  * Sixteen – 1 1/2" x 1 3/4" (A4a, A5a, B4a, B5a)
- One 1 1/2" wide strip. From this, cut:
  * Sixteen – 1 1/2" sq. (A7a, A8a, B7a, B8a)

ASSEMBLY

Making Block A.

1. Use diagonal corner technique to make two each of units 9 and 10. Use this technique to make one each of units 7, 8, and 13.

2. Use diagonal end technique to make units 4 and 5 as shown

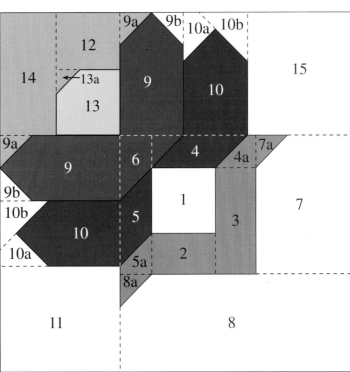

Block A. Make 4. Finishes to: 11" square

below.

3. Refer to illustration below to make unit 10. Units 9 and 10 are made in the same manner for Block B.

4. We have given you step-by-step illustrations showing how to make the center section for both Block A and Block B. It is made in a "log cabin" manner. Refer to these illustrations on the next page for easy assembly.

Making Unit 4 for Blocks A and B

| 4 | 4a | | 4 | 4a |

Making Unit 5 for Blocks A and B

| 5a | 5 | | 5a | 5 |

Making Unit 10 for Block A

| 10a | | 10a | | 10a | 10b | | 10a | 10b |
| 10 | | 10 | | 10 | | 10 |

Step 1   Step 2

5. To make center section, begin by joining units 1 and 2; then add Unit 3 to right side. Join Unit 4 to top; then add Unit 5 to left side as shown. Use Unit 6 square as a diagonal corner and add to the combined units as shown.

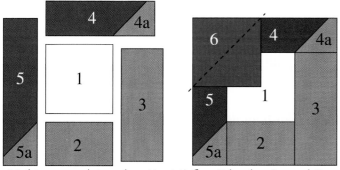

Making combined units 1-5 for Blocks A and B

Making Block B

1. Use diagonal corner technique to make two each of units 9 and 10 as illustrated on page 13. Use this technique to make one each of units 7, 8, 11, 13, and 15.

2. Use diagonal end technique to make one each of units 4 and 5 as illustrated on page 13.

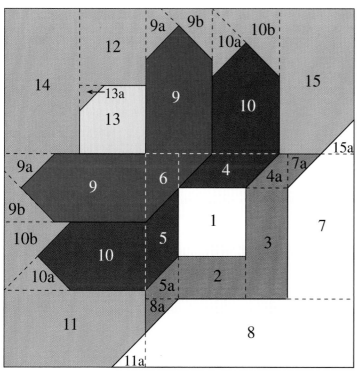

Block B. Make 4. Finishes to: 10 1/2" square

Assembly For Blocks A and B.

1. Both A and B blocks are assembled in the same manner. You will begin with the center section. Refer to Step 5 above and illustrations.

2. After center section is assembled, join Unit 7 to right side of center section; then add Unit 8 to bottom. Referring to top of block, join units 9, 10 and 15 in a row as shown. Add this row to top of center section.

3. Join units 12 and 13; then add Unit 14 to left side of combined units. Join remaining units 9, 10, and 11 in a row and add to combined units 12-14. Join this section to left side of other completed section to complete the blocks.

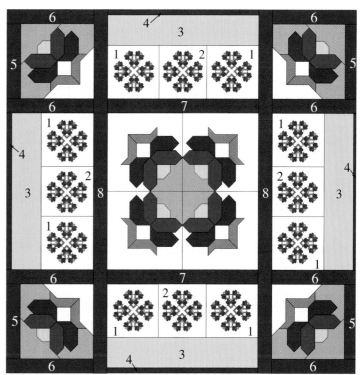

Finishes to 51" square

Tablecloth Top Assembly.

1. To assemble the top, begin by joining the four A blocks together as shown, matching seams. Join Unit Q7 to top and bottom of combined A blocks.

2. Join embroidered Q1 and Q2 blocks together as shown. Make four of these embroidered block rows. Join units 3 and 4; then add to the bottom of the embroidered block rows as illustrated.

3. Refer to illustration above for correct placement, and join Unit Q5 to one side of Block B. Join Unit 6 to opposite sides of Block B as illustrated.

4. Again referring to illustration above, join Block B to top and bottom of two combined 1-4 sections, making certain that Block B is facing in the correct direction.

5. Join the two remaining 1-4 sections to top and bottom of center Block A section.

6. Join Unit Q8 to sides of Block A center section as shown; then add the assembled Block B side sections to opposite sides of center section to complete the top.

Quilting And Finishing

1. Stitch in the ditch around all patchwork and embroideries. Faye used a variety of tulip quilting motifs on the patchwork tablecloth, placed at the corners of Block B, and on Unit Q3. She also added tulips around the center A blocks.

2. If the Q1 and Q2 units are not embroidered, use a tulip design to quilt in that space.

3. Use approximately 215" of straight-grain French-fold binding to bind your tablecloth.

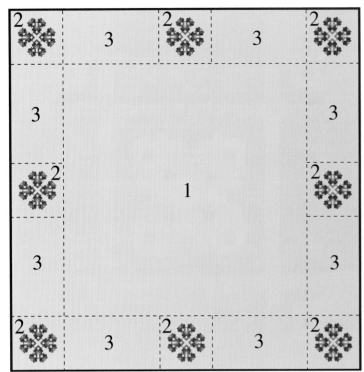

Tulip Undercloth finishes to 60" square.

Embroidered place mats and napkins illustrated below show the measurements that we used and suggested fabric colors for the design. We used French-fold binding on both the place mats and the napkins.

Napkins are made by embroidering the small tulip on one corner of the napkin as shown. 12 1/2" squares were cut of two different fabrics for the reversible napkin. Upon completion of the embroidery, cut 1 1/2" from side edge of embroidery to napkin edge; then square off to 12 1/2". Place the two 12 1/2" squares for the napkins wrong sides together and bind with French-fold binding. This takes a while to do, but we love the results. Two kinds of napkin folds are shown; one in the illustration, and one in the photo. These folds make convenient pockets in which to place the silverware. If you choose to make napkin rings, we suggest making them from a fabric used in the place mat for balance of color.

For suggested napkin folds, refer to pages 34, 62, and 96.

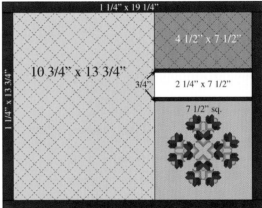

Place mat finishes to 14 3/4" x 18 3/4"   12" square napkins.

You will need:
130 1/2" of small gold check - 3 3/4 yards
From this you will cut:
- One 42 1/2" square (Q1)
- Three 18" wide strips. From these, cut:
    * Eight - 12" x 16" for embroideries (Q2). Upon completion of embroideries, center embroideries and cut down to 9 1/2" squares.
- Two 17" wide strips. From these, cut:
    * Eight - 9 1/2" x 17" (Q3)

You will need:
15" of dark red print - 1/2 yard.
From this you will cut:
- Six 2 1/2" wide strips for straight grain binding.

To Assemble:
Join units Q3, Q2, and Q3 in a row. Make four. Add two to opposite sides of 42 1/2" square. Add remaining units Q2 to opposite ends of remaining Q3, Q2, Q3 combination. Join these to top and bottom of center section to complete undercloth.

The quilted tulip motifs were carried onto the undercloth, using larger tulips in the center with swirls, and the smaller tulips around the outer edges.

Use approximately 250" of straight-grain French-fold binding to bind your tablecloth.

Field of Daisies

Summer in Colorado is a part of my artistic soul. Each week of summer brings a new flower. As one fades away, another takes its place, giving fresh inspiration and renewed color.

By mid July, no matter what we are doing, we set it aside and head for the high country in our 4-wheel drive vehicles. Mother Earth has painted an extraordinary picture there. Although there are existing paintings and photo's, the true depth of it all can not be captured on canvas or film. Meadows of thousands of flowers, their names and colors too numerous to mention are spread before us, arranged perfectly. We feel that centuries of thought and toil have been spent in the planting of this garden by a master artist, the palette overflowing with colors and textures.

Daisies appear in August, and our trip to the mountains with our friend Pat's bed, and our quilts in tow was a joyous task for our entire crew. The photo's were taken in the first meadow on Old Lime Creek trail, and we felt it appropriate to include our Old English Sheepdog, "Little Bear" who is the great, great grandson of the Sheepdog cast in the movie "Please Don't Eat The Daisies." "Bear" felt very much at home as you can see!

Enjoy!
Pam & Little Bear

Field Of Daisies quilt finishes to: 100" x 108"
Block A finishes to 8" square.

For Embroidered Accessories:

Robison Anton #40 weight rayon embroidery thread: #2534
Salem Blue (dk. blue), #2275 Slate Blue (medium blue), #2522
Bridgeport Blue (lt. Blue), #2250 Pistachio (green), #2493 Lt.
Bronze (dk. gold), #2606 TH Gold (medium gold), and #2732
Pro Maize (yellow).

> Techniques used: Diagonal Corners, Diagonal Ends,
> Half Square Triangles, and Strip Sets.

MATERIALS FOR QUILT

☐	Fabric I (unbleached muslin)	Need 215 1/2"	6 1/8 yards
■	Fabric II (navy print)	Need 72"	2 1/8 yards
■	Fabric III (medium blue print)	Need 54 3/4"	1 5/8 yards
■	Fabric IV (gold print)	Need 65 3/4"	2 yards
■	Fabric V (light blue print)	Need 30 1/2"	1 yard
■	Fabric VI (light olive print)	Need 36 1/2"	1 1/8 yards
■	Fabric VII (dark olive print)	Need 12 1/2"	1/2 yard
	Backing		9 yards

CUTTING

All "Q" units in cutting instructions stand for "quilt top." These are units that are not incorporated into the specific blocks, but are on the quilt top.

Cutting instructions shown in red indicate that the quantity of units is combined and cut in 2 or more different places to conserve fabric.

☐ **From Fabric I, cut: (unbleached muslin)**
- Three 8 1/2" wide strips. From these, cut:
  * Two - 8 1/2" x 40 1/2" (Q22)
  * One - 8 1/2" x 32 1/2" (Q25)
- From scrap, cut:
  * Fifty-four - 1 1/4" squares (A1c, A2a, A3b, A4a, A5a, A7b, A9b)
- Two 5" wide strips. From these, cut:
  * Forty-two - 2" x 5" (A9a)
- One 4 1/2" wide strip. From this, cut:
  * Four - 4 1/2" x 8 1/2" (Q10)

- Two 3 1/2" wide strips. From these, cut:
  * Forty-two - 2" x 3 1/2" (A7a)
- Fifty-nine - 2 1/2" wide strips. Twenty-six for Strip Sets 1, 2, and 3. From remaining thirty-three strips, cut:
  * Two - 2 1/2" x 42" (Q20)
  * Four - 2 1/2" x 27 3./4" (Q20) Piece Q20 strips together to = two 96 1/2" lengths
  * One - 2 1/2" x 42" (Q27)
  * Two - 2 1/2" x 29 3/4" (Q27) Piece Q27 strips together to = one 100 1/2" length.
  * Two - 2 1/2" x 42" (Q24)
  * Four - 2 1/2" x 28 3/4" (Q24) Piece Q24 strips together to = two 98 1/2" lengths.
  * Two - 2 1/2" x 40 1/2" (Q21) Piece together to = 80 1/2" length.
  * Four - 2 1/2" x 32 1/2" (Q7)
  * Eight - 2 1/2" x 28 3/4" (Q11) Piece together to = four 56 1/2" lengths.
  * Twelve - 2 1/2" x 12 1/2" (Q8)
  * Twelve - 2 1/2" x 8 1/2" (Q9, Q23, Q26)

* Seventy-four- 2 1/2" squares (A6, checkerboard corners)
- Three 2" wide strips. From these, cut:
  * Eighty-four - 1 1/4" x 2" (A8)
  * Eighteen - 1 1/4" squares (Add to 1 1/4" sq. above)
- Twelve 1 1/4" wide strips. From these cut:
  * 390 - 1 1/4" squares (Add to 1 1/4" sq. above)

From Fabric II, cut: (navy print)
- Twenty-four 2 1/2" wide strips. Five strips for Strip Sets 1, 2, and 3. From remaining nineteen strips, cut:
  * Two - 2 1/2" x 42" (Q16)
  * Four - 2 1/2" x 24 3/4" (Q16) Piece Q16 strips together to = two 90 1/2" lengths.
  * Four - 2 1/2" x 41 1/2" (Q14) Piece together to = two 82 1/2" lengths.
  * Four - 2 1/2" x 37 1/2" (Q17) Piece together to = two 74 1/2" lengths.
  * Four - 2 1/2" x 33 1/2" (Q15) Piece together to = two 66 1/2" lengths.
  * Forty - 2 1/2" x 2 3/4" (A5)
  * Four - 2 1/2" squares (checkerboard corners)
- Three 2 3/4" wide strips. From these, cut:
  * Two - 2 /12" x 2 3/4" (Add to A5 above)
  * Forty-two - 2 3/4" squares (A3a)
- Three 1 1/4" wide strips. From these, cut:
  * Eighty-four - 1 1/4" squares (A1b A2b)

From Fabric III, cut: (medium blue print)
- Five 4 3/4" wide strips. From these, cut:
  * Sixty-eight - 2 3/4" x 4 3/4" (A2, A4)
  * Four - 2 1/2" squares (checkerboard corners)
- Six 3 1/2" wide strips. From these, cut:
  * Two - 3 1/2" x 28 1/2" (Q3)
  * Four - 3 1/2" x 27 1/2" (Q4) Piece together to = two 54 1/2" lengths.
  * Sixteen - 2 3/4" x 4 3/4" (add to A2, A4)
- Four 2 1/2" wide strips for Strip Sets 1, 2, and 3.

From Fabric IV, cut: (gold print)
- Three 2 3/4" wide strips. From these, cut:
  * Forty-two - 2 3/4" squares (A1)
- Five 2 1/2" wide strips. Four for Strip Sets 1, 2, and 3. From remaining strip, cut:
  * Eight - 2 1/2" squares (checkerboard corners)
- Thirty 1 1/2" wide strips. From these, cut:
  * Two - 1 1/2" x 42" (Q18)
  * Four - 1 1/2" x 26 3/4" (Q18) Piece Q18 strips together to = two 94 1/2" lengths.
  * Four - 1 1/2" x 40 1/2" (Q12) Piece together to = two 80 1/2" lengths.
  * Four - 1 1/2" x 38 1/2" (Q19) Piece together to = two 76 1/2" lengths.
  * Four - 1 1/2" x 31 1/2" (Q13) Piece together to = two 62 1/2" lengths.
  * Two - 1 1/2" x 34 1/2" (Q5)
  * Four - 1 1/2" x 28 1/2" (Q6) Piece together to = two 56 1/2" lengths.
  * Two - 1 1/2" x 26 1/2" (Q1)
  * Four - 1 1/2" x 24 1/2" (Q2) Piece together to = two 48 1/2" lengths.

From Fabric V, cut: (light blue print)
- Three 4 3/4" wide strips. From these, cut:
  * Forty-two - 2 3/4" x 4 3/4" (A3)
  * Twenty-one - 1 1/4" squares (A1b, A4c)
- Six 2 1/2" wide strips. Five for Strip Sets 1, 2, and 3. From remaining strip, cut:
  * Four - 2 1/2" squares (checkerboard corners)
  * Fifty - 1 1/4" squares (Add to A1b, A4c)
- One 1 1/4" wide strip. From this, cut:
  * Thirteen - 1 1/4" squares (Add to A1b, A4c)

From Fabric VI, cut: (light olive print)
- Four 4 3/4" wide strips. From these, cut:
  * Eighty-four - 2" x 4 3/4" (A7, A9)
- Five 2 1/2" wide strips. Four for Strip Sets 1, 2, and 3. From remaining strip, cut:
  * Four - 2 1/2" squares (checkerboard corners)
  * Fifty - 1 1/4" squares (A1a, A2c, A4b)
- Four 1 1/4" wide strips. From these, cut:
  * 118 - 1 1/4" squares (Add to A1a, A2c, A4b)

From Fabric VII, cut: (dark olive print)
- Five 2 1/2" wide strips. Four for Strip Sets 1, 2, and 3. From remaining strip, cut:
  * Eight - 2 1/2" squares (checkerboard corners)

ASSEMBLY

Making The Strip Sets.
1. Refer to illustration of strip sets below. Each strip is 2 1/2" wide and is indicated in the cutting list. As you will be joining thirteen strips together for each strip set, you will want to use anti-directional sewing as explained on page 7. Join the strips as shown below. Taking into consideration the way the strip sets will be joined in the quilt center, if all seams are pressed towards the dark strips, the seams should interlock when the strip sets are joined together. Cut the strip sets into segments as shown below.
2. Mark large zip top bags and place all like strip sets together in the bags for easy identification. This quilt has strip sets identified

Strip Sets For Quilt:
All strips are 2 1/2" wide. Strip sets should measure 26 1/2" unfinished.

Strip Set 1. Make 1. Cut into 8 - 2 1/2" segments.

Strip Set 2. Make 2. Cut into 19 - 2 1/2" segments

Strip Set 3. Make 1. Cut into 9 - 2 1/2" segments

on the quilt center assembly diagram for easy placement.

Making Block A
1. Refer to diagrams below, and read instructions in gold box for making Unit 1b. When stitched as a diagonal corner onto Unit 1, triangle square 1b will be placed right sides together on Unit 1, and sewn as shown.
2. Use diagonal corner technique to make one each of units 1, 2, 3, 4, and 5.

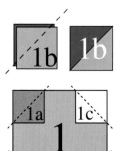

Use this assembly for Block A, Unit 1b.

Place 1 1/4" squares of fabrics II and V right sides together, matching raw edges, and stitch a diagonal line down the center as shown. Press open and trim center seam, leaving the top and base fabric.

You now have a triangle-square which will be used as a diagonal corner as shown at left. Place it on the main Unit 1 and stitch in place as shown.

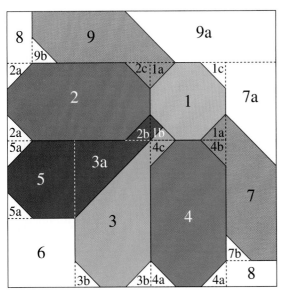

Make 42 for quilt. Make 12 for table topper, and make 4 for pillow.

Block A

3. Use diagonal end technique to make one each of units 7 and 9, shown at right. Add diagonal corners 7b and 9b after completion of diagonal ends.

4. To assemble the block, begin by joining units 1 and 2. Join units 3 and 4. Join units 5 and 6; then add them to the left side of combined units 3-4. Join combined units 1-2 to top of combined units 3-6.

Making Unit 9 for Block A

Making Unit 7 for Block A

5. Join Unit 8 to bottom of Unit 7; then add to right side of daisy combined units. Join remaining Unit 8 to Unit 9; then add to top of other combined units to complete Block A. Make 42 of Block A for the quilt.

Making The Strip Set Quilt Center

1. Refer to illustration of the strip set center of the quilt. Begin joining the strip set rows as shown. If strips have been pressed as directed in Step 1 of Making The Strip Sets, seams should interlock, making it easy to match the corners of each square.
2. Take note of the colors shown when joining the strip sets as some of them are turned to make best use of color placement.
3. When all of the strip sets are joined, add Unit Q1 to top and bottom of strip set center as shown; then add Unit Q2 to opposite sides. Join Unit Q3 to top of bottom of center section; then join Unit Q4 to opposite sides. Join Unit Q5 to top and bottom of center section; then join Unit Q6 to opposite sides to complete quilt top center.

Completing The Quilt Top

1. Refer to quilt top illustration on page 22 to add units and blocks correctly. To complete the quilt top, begin by joining four of Block A together, matching the leaves as shown. Pin seams to assure a good match. Make two of these combined block sections. Join Unit Q7 to top and bottom; then add Unit Q8 to sides. Join these completed block sections to top and bottom of center section.
2. You have cut 2 1/2" squares from all of the fabrics for the checkerboard corners. All of the checkerboard corners are the same, they are just turned differently. Refer to the quilt top illustration showing the corners for proper placement of the squares. Once again, press seams toward the darkest fabric and seams should interlock when you sew the rows together. Join the rows as shown and make 4 sets of corners.
3. Join Unit Q9 to opposite sides of each checkerboard corner, referring frequently to quilt top diagram for correct placement. Join Unit Q8 to remaining opposite sides of each corner.
4. Join six of Block A together, matching the leaves as shown in diagram. Make two of these combined block sections. Join Unit Q10 to both short sides of each block section. Join Unit Q11 to opposite long sides of each block section.

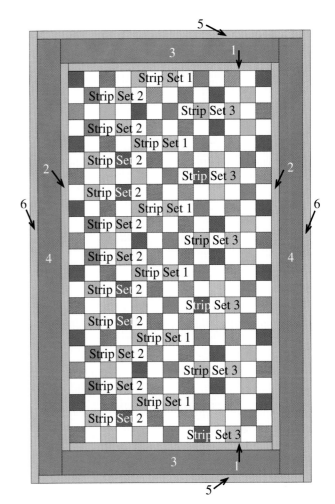

STRIP SET QUILT TOP CENTER

5. Join the checkerboard corners (referring to diagram for correct placement of color) to opposite short ends of the block sections, matching Unit Q8 and Q11 seams. Join to opposite sides of quilt top. Add Unit Q12 strips to opposite sides of quilt top as shown; then join strip Unit Q13 to top and bottom.
6. Join Fabric II borders (Q14) to opposite sides of quilt top; then join borders Q15 to top and bottom.
7. For checked borders, strip sets are used. You will have to remove some squares from some of the strip sets as shown on the quilt top illustration on page 22. The top and bottom borders will be added first, so they will begin and end with a Fabric I square of Strip Set 2. Join strip sets together as shown for top and bottom borders. Join combined strip sets to top and bottom of quilt top.
8. Some squares must be removed from Strip Set 2 for the checked sides. Refer to drawing on page 22 and remove the squares. Join the strip sets and add to the sides of the quilt top.
9. Join borders (Q16) to opposite sides of quilt; then add Q17 borders to top and bottom. Join Q18 border strips to opposite sides; then join Q19 border strips to top and bottom. Join previously pieced Q20 borders to opposite sides of quilt top; then add Q21 to bottom as shown.
10. Join four of Block A for top of side section of border as shown. Make 2. Add Unit Q22 to one end, and Unit Q23 to other end. Join three of Block A as shown, checking to make sure they are in the correct position. Add them to the bottom of Unit Q22. Refer to diagram for placement, and join Unit Q24 to one long side of each Block A border section. Join this Block A border to opposite sides of quilt top as shown.
11. For bottom row, join four of Block A as shown. Make two sets, making sure they are facing the right direction so that they make the "curve" when joined to the quilt bottom. Join Unit Q25 between them, and Unit Q26 to opposite short ends. Add to quilt bottom. Join Unit Q27 to quilt bottom.

Finishes to 100" x 108"

QUILTING AND FINISHING

The quilting on this piece is exquisite. As we wanted to shoot photography in the summer when the daisies were in bloom, this was the first quilt that was made. I told Faye that I wanted it "Dripping with quilting!" It is!

She ditched the patchwork and used a medium stipple on all of the other areas, but threw in gorgeous swirling feather designs on larger areas, especially the borders.

Although it looks as though it was planned, when you look at the photo, you will notice how the quilting works beautifully on our friend Pat's bed, especially in the front. This was a splendid surprise when we put the quilt on the bed in the meadow. It intensified my feelings regarding the fact that quilting should be planned out as much as the patchwork is planned taking into consideration the bed on which a large quilt will be placed.

For the binding, we used approximately 425" of 2 1/2" wide straight-grain binding, however we joined remaining strip sets, made a few more to give the correct amount, and used them for the binding. It gives a terrific effect. Give it a try!

FIELD OF DAISIES TABLE TOPPER

Finishes to: 54" square
Block A finishes to: 8" square.
Techniques used: Diagonal Corners, Diagonal Ends, and Half Square Triangles.

MATERIALS FOR TABLE TOPPER

Fabric I (muslin)	Need 58 1/4"	1 3/4 yards
Fabric II (navy print)	Need 8"	1/4 yard
Fabric III (med. blue print)	Need 39 3/4"	1 1/4 yards
Fabric IV (gold print)	Need 15 3/4"	1/2 yard
Fabric V (lt. blue print)	Need 7 1/4"	1/4 yard
Fabric VI (lt. olive print)	Need 9 1/2"	3/8 yard
Fabric VII (dark olive print)	Need 5"	1/4 yard
Backing		3 1/2 yards

CUTTING

From Fabric I, cut: (muslin)
• Two 8 1/2" wide strips. From these, cut:
  * Eight - 5 1/2" x 8 1/2" (Q9)
  * Twelve - 2" x 5" (A9a)
  * Twelve - 2" x 3 1/2" (A7a)
  * Twenty-four - 1 1/4" x 2" (A8)
  * Twenty - 1 1/4" squares (A1c, A2a, A3b, A4a, A5a, A7b, A9b)
• Fifteen 2 1/2" wide strips. From these, cut:
  * Two - 2 1/2" x 34 1/2" (Q8)
  * Two - 2 1/2" x 30 1/2" (Q7)
  * Four - 2 1/2" x 27 1/2" (Q11) Piece together to = two 54 1/2" lengths.
  * Four - 2 1/2" x 25 1/2" (Q10) Piece together to = two 50 1/2" lengths.
  * Ninety-four- 2 1/2" squares (A6, checkerboards)
  * Twenty-six - 1 1/4" squares (Add to 1 1/4" sq. above)
• Three 1 1/4" wide strips. From these, cut:
  * Eighty-six - 1 1/4" squares (Add to 1 1/4" sq. above)

From Fabric I1, cut: (navy print)
• Two 2 3/4" wide strips. From these, cut:
  * Twelve - 2 3/4" squares (A3a)
  * Twelve - 2 1/2" x 2 3/4" (A5)
  * Seven - 2 1/2" squares (checkerboards)
• One 2 1/2" wide strip. From this, cut:
  * Seven - 2 1/2" squares (add to checkerboards)
  * Twenty-four - 1 1/4" squares (A1b, A2b)

From Fabric III, cut: (medium blue print)
• Four 3 1/2" wide strips. From these, cut:
  * Two - 3 1/2" x 28 1/2" (Q4)
  * Two - 3 1/2: x 22 1/2" (Q3)
• Three 2 3/4" wide strips. From these, cut:
  * Twenty-four - 2 3/4" x 4 3/4" (A2, A4)
• Seven 2 1/2" wide strips. Six strips for binding.
From remaining strip, cut:
  * Thirteen - 2 1/2" squares (checkerboards)

From Fabric IV, cut: (gold print)
• One 2 3/4" wide strip. From this, cut:
  * Twelve - 2 3/4" squares (A1)
  * Three - 2 1/2" squares (checkerboard blocks)
• One 2 1/2" wide strip. From this, cut:
  * Fifteen - 2 1/2" squares (add to checkerboard blocks)
• Seven 1 1/2" wide strips. From these, cut:
  * Two - 1 1/2" x 30 1/2" (Q6)
  * Two - 1 1/2" x 28 1/2" (Q5)
  * Two - 1 1/2" x 22 1/2" (Q2)
  * Two - 1 1/2" x 20 1/2" (Q1)

From Fabric V, cut: (light blue print)
• One 4 3/4" wide strip. From this, cut:
  * Twelve - 2 3/4" x 4 3/4" (A3)
  * Twenty-one - 1 1/4" squares (A1b, A4c)
• One 2 1/2" wide strip. From this, cut:
  * Eleven - 2 1/2" squares (checkerboards)
  * Three - 1 1/4" squares (Add to A1b and A4c above)

From Fabric VI, cut: (light olive print)
• Two 4 3/4" wide strips. From these, cut:
  * Twenty-four - 2" x 4 3/4" (A7, A9)
  * Eight - 2 1/2" squares (checkerboards)
  * Forty-eight - 1 1/4" squares (A1a, A2c, and A4b)

From Fabric VII, cut: (dark olive print)
• Two 2 1/2" wide strips. From these, cut:
  * Eighteen - 2 1/2" squares (checkerboards)

ASSEMBLY

1. Refer to instructions and diagrams on pages 20 and 21 for making Block A. Make twelve of Block A for the table topper.
2. Our cutting instructions give you the correct amount of 2 1/2" squares of each fabric for all of the checkerboards. We did a mix of colors on the center section. Refer to this section for correct placement of fabrics and join them together into rows. Join the 10 rows together as shown.
3. The small checkerboard blocks are all the same. Refer to colors shown and make four of these smaller blocks.
4. To assemble the table topper, begin by adding border Q1 to top and bottom of checkerboard center section; then join border Q2 to opposite sides. Add border Q3 to top and bottom; then join border Q4 to opposite sides as shown. Join border Q5 to top and bottom of center section; then join border Q6 to opposite sides. Join Q7, border to top an bottom of center section; then add border Q8 to opposite sides.
5. Referring to illustration on page 24, you will be adding the top and bottom Block A border sections first. Make sure that Block A daisies are facing correctly. Join Unit Q9 to opposite sides of small checkerboard block. Make four and set two aside. Add one of Block A to each short end. Make 2 and join them to top and bottom of center section.
6. For side borders, join two of Block A together, referring to diagram for correct placement. Make four of these combined blocks and join them to opposite short sides of Unit Q9. Add to opposite sides of table topper. Join previously pieced Unit 10 to top and bottom of table topper; then add Unit Q11 to sides.

QUILTING AND FINISHING

Quilting on the table topper is the same as on the quilt, with medium stippling and feathers.

For the binding, we used approximately 225" of 2 1/2" wide straight-grain binding cut from Fabric III.

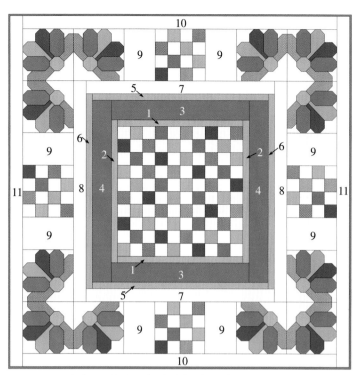

FIELD OF DAISIES TABLE TOPPER

DRESSER SCARF ASSEMBLY

1. Join the checkerboard 2 1/2" squares in the center as shown. Join Unit Q3 to top and bottom of checkerboard center; then add Unit Q4 to opposite sides.
2. Join Unit Q1 to top and bottom of checkerboard. Add embroidered daisy to opposite short ends of remaining Q1 units; then join to sides of dresser scarf.
3. Join Unit Q5 to top and bottom of dresser scarf; then add Unit Q6 to sides to complete.
4. Cut a 15 1/2" square of the backing of your choice. To quilt the piece, we used a 15 1/2" square of flannel for the batting Layer as follows: Flannel, backing face up, dresser scarf top face down. Pin layers together. Begin in the center of one side and using 1/4" seam, stitch around outer edge, leaving about a 3" opening to turn.
5. Turn right side out, press, and slip stitch opening closed. Quilt as desired.

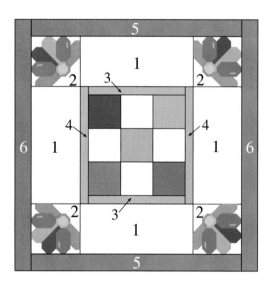

FIELD OF DAISIES DRESSER SCARF
Finishes to: 15" square.

MATERIALS FOR DRESSER SCARF

Muslin - 12 1/4"   1/2 yard

Gold print - 2 1/2"   1/8 yard

Dk. olive print - 18 1/2"   5/8 yard

Scraps of: navy print, med. blue print and lt. blue print.

CUTTING FOR DRESSER SCARF

From muslin, cut:
• One 8 3/4" wide strip. From this, cut:
    * Four – 8 3/4" x 10 1/2" (Q2 for 100 x 100 mm embroidery hoop). After 3" embroidery is complete, center daisy and cut each to 3 1/2" squares.
• One 3 1/2" wide strip. From this, cut:
    * Four - 3 1/2" x 7 1/2" (Q1)
    * Four - 2 1/2" squares (checkerboard)

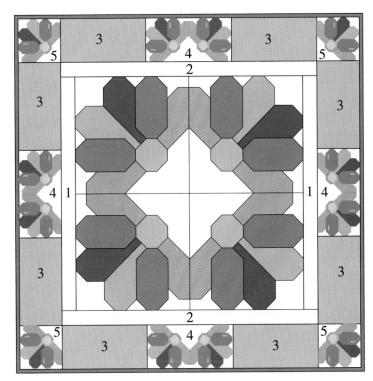

Embroidered pillow. Finishes to 24" square

MATERIALS FOR 24" SQUARE PILLOW

☐	Fabric I (muslin)	Need 49 1/2"	1 1/2 yards
■	Fabric II (navy print)	Need 2 3/4"	1/8 yard
■	Fabric III (med. blue print)	Need 42 1/2"	1 1/4 yards
▨	Fabric IV (gold print)	Need 7"	1/4 yard
▨	Fabric V (lt. blue print)	Need 2 3/4"	1/8 yard
▨	Fabric VI (lt. olive print)	Need 3 1/4"	1/4 yard

CUTTING FOR 24" SQUARE PILLOW

☐ **From Fabric I, cut: (muslin)**
- Two 16" wide strips. From these, cut:
  * Four – 12" x 16" (Q4 for 150 x 240mm embroidery hoop) After embroideries are completed, center double daisies and cut each to 3 1/2" x 6 1/2".
- One 8 3/4" wide strip. From this, cut:
  * Four – 8 3/4" x 10 1/2" (Q5 for 100 x 100 mm embroidery hoop). Embroideries should measure 3" square. After they are completed, center daisy and cut each to 3 1/2" squares.
- One 2 1/2" wide strip. From this, cut:
  * Four - 2 1/2" squares (A6)
  * Forty-four - 1 1/4" squares (A1c, A2a, A3b, A4a, A5a, A7b, A9b)
- One 2" wide strip. From this, cut:
  * Four - 2" x 5" (A9a)
  * Four - 2" x 3 1/2" (A7a)
- Two 1 1/2" wide strips. From these, cut:
  * Two - 1 1/2" x 18 1/2" (Q2)
  * Two – 1 1/2" x 16 1/2" (Q1)
- One 1 1/4" wide strip. From this, cut:
  * Eight - 1 1/4" x 2" (A8)

■ **From Fabric II, cut: (navy print)**
- One 2 3/4" wide strip. From this, cut:
  * Four - 2 3/4" squares (A3a)
  * Four - 2 1/2" x 2 3/4" (A5)
  * Eight - 1 1/4" squares (A1b, A2b)

■ **From Fabric III, cut: (medium blue print)**
- 1/2 yard to cut 2" wide bias strips for cording.
- One 24 1/2" wide strip. From this, cut:
  * Two - 15 1/2" x 24 1/2" (pillow backing)
  * Eight - 2 3/4" x 4 3/4" (A2, A4)

▨ **From Fabric IV, cut: (gold print)**
- Two 3 1/2" wide strips. From these, cut:
  * Eight - 3 1/2" x 6 1/2" (Q3)
  * Four - 2 3/4" squares (A1)

▨ **From Fabric V, cut: (light blue print)**
- One 2 3/4" wide strip. From this, cut:
  * Four - 2 3/4" x 4 3/4" (A3)
  * Eight - 1 1/4" squares (A1b, A4c)

▨ **From Fabric VI, cut: (light olive print)**
- One 2" wide strip. From this, cut:
  * Eight - 2" x 4 3/4" (A7, A9)
- One 1 1/4" wide strip. From this, cut:
  * Sixteen - 1 1/4" squares (A1a, A2c, A4b)

ASSEMBLY

1. Refer to instructions and diagrams on pages 20 and 21 for making Block A. Make four of Block A. Refer to pillow illustration, and join the four blocks together as shown.

2. Join Unit Q1 to opposite sides of center; then add Unit 2 to top and bottom. Add Unit Q3 to both short sides of all four embroidered double daisies. Join two of these to opposite sides of pillow top. Join single daisies to opposite short sides of remaining two. Add them to top and bottom of pillow top.

3. To finish your pillow press under 1/4"twice on one 24 1/2" side of each pillow backing. Top stitch in place. Place the two pillow backs face down on pillow front, overlapping hemmed edges, and pin. Use 1/4" seam and stitch around outer edge of pillow. Turn right side out to complete.

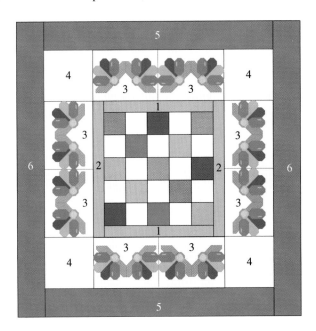

Embroidered flange pillow. Center finishes to 21" square. Finished size with flange: 26" sq.

MATERIALS FOR EMBROIDERED FLANGE PILLOW

☐	Fabric I (muslin)	Need 48"	1 1/2 yard
■	Fabric II (navy print)	Need 2 1/2"	1/8 yard
▨	Fabric III (med. blue print)	Need 38 1/2"	1 1/8 yards
▤	Fabric IV (gold print)	Need 3"	1/8 yard

Scraps of lt. blue print, lt. olive print, and dark olive print.

CUTTING

☐ **From Fabric I, cut: (muslin)**
• Three 16" wide strips. From these, cut:
 * Eight – 12" x 16" (Q3 for 150 x 240mm embroidery hoop) After embroidery is complete, center double daisies and cut each to 5" x 6 1/2".
• From scrap, cut:
 * Four – 5" sq. (Q4)
 * Twelve - 2 1/2" squares (checkerboard)

■ **From Fabric II, cut: (navy print)**
• One 2 1/2" wide strip. From this, cut:
 * Three - 2 1/2" squares (checkerboard)

▨ **From Fabric III, cut: (med. blue print)**
• One 26 1/2" wide strip. From this, cut:
 * Two – 16 1/2" x 26 1/2" (pillow backing)
• Four 3" wide strips. From these, cut:
 * Two - 3" x 21 1/2" (Q5)
 * Two - 3" x 26 1/2" (Q6)
 * Two - 2 1/2" squares (checkerboard)

▤ **From Fabric IV, cut: (gold print)**
• One 3" wide strip. From this, cut:
 * Two - 2 1/2" squares (checkerboard)
• Cut remainder of strip down to two 1 1/2" wide strips. From these, cut:
 * Two - 1 1/2" x 10 1/2" (Q1)
 * Two - 1 1/2" x 12 1/2" (Q2)

From scraps of lt. blue and lt. olive, and dk. olive, cut 2 each 2 1/2" squares.

ASSEMBLY

1. Refer to diagram on page 25 of flange pillow. To assemble, begin by joining the cut 2 1/2" squares for the checkerboard. Join together in 5 rows; then join the rows. Pressing seams to the darkest fabric will help in the piecing, as seams will interlock.

2. After completion of checkerboard center, join units Q1 to top and bottom; then add Q2 units to opposite sides.

3. Care should be taken when joining the Q3 embroidered blocks so that embroidered petals match. Refer to illustration and join four sets of two blocks each. Join two of the sets to top and bottom of pillow center as shown. Join Unit Q4 to opposite short ends of remaining two sets; then add them to pillow sides, matching corner seams.

4. Join Unit Q5 to top and bottom of pillow; then join Unit Q6 to opposite sides.

5. Press under 1/4" twice on 26 1/2" side of each pillow backing. Top stitch in place. Place the two pillow backs face down on pillow front, overlapping hemmed edges, and pin. Use 1/4" seam and stitch around outer edge of pillow. Turn right side out and press.

6. After pressing top, pin, along Fabric III flange seam lines and top stitch with coordinating thread through all thicknesses.

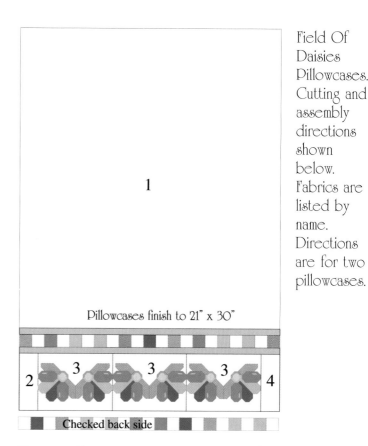

Field Of Daisies Pillowcases. Cutting and assembly directions shown below. Fabrics are listed by name. Directions are for two pillowcases.

Pillowcases finish to 21" x 30"

From muslin, cut: (you will need 96" - 1 7/8 yards)
• Two 24" x 42 1/2" strips for Q1.
• Two 7 1/2" x 42 1/2" strips for border lining.
• Three 16" wide strips. From these, cut twelve 12" x 16" for Q3 embroideries. Instructions are same as for flange pillow.
• From scrap, cut:
 * Two – 3 1/2" x 5" (Q4), Four – 2" x 5" (Q2), and Forty-two – 1 1/2" sq. (for checked border).

From gold print, cut: (you will need 5 1/2" - 1/4 yard)
• One 1 1/2" wide strip. From this, cut:
 * Eight – 1 1/2" sq. for checked border.
• Four - 1" x 42 1/2" (sashing border)

Checked border, cut: (5" sq. scraps work for each color)
Eight 1 1/2" squares of light blue print and light olive print. Six 1 1/2" squares of navy print, medium blue print, and dark olive print.

ASSEMBLY

1. Refer to illustration above and join forty-two 1 1/2" squares in a row as shown. Add the gold print sashing strips to opposite long sides of the joined checked print; then add to muslin pillowcase bottom.

2. The embroidered borders are joined in three's as shown. Three for the front, and three for the back. Join Unit Q4 between the joined rows for each pillowcase and join Unit Q2 to each short end. Join this embroidered row to bottom of pillowcase.

3. Join the lining strips to embroidered pillowcase bottom and press the seam towards the embroidered border.

4. Fold the pillowcase in half, right sides together, and serge or use overcast stitch around 2 sides, leaving bottom open. Turn right side out and press under 1/4" hem. Press the lining up inside. Turn pillowcase wrong side out, and whip stitch the lining in place. Lining should cover raw seams of border.

Rose of Sharon Quilt

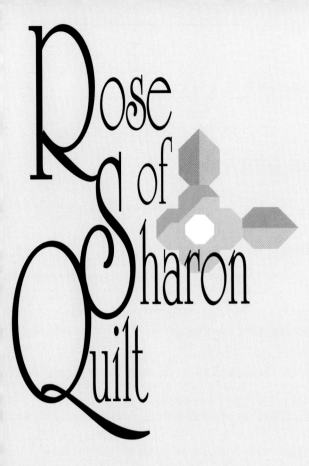

The inspiration for this quilt was given to me one evening when I attended a surprise birthday party at the home of a lovely lady.

The quilts that adorned her walls and beds were of such delicate perfection and artistry, that I could not help but admire each one as I was invited to tour her delightful home in the mountains.

Tastefully placed on a day bed in her studio was a quilt that I could not take my eyes from. I returned several times during the evening to admire it.

Although simple in design, the elegance came from crochet doilies that were appliquéd on the quilt top. During dinner conversation, I learned that the doilies had been crocheted by the lady's mother, giving the quilt a special significance, filled with joyful memories to be treasured by her entire family.

When we were in the planning stages for this book, my mind continued to return to the doily quilt, and the love that had been put into each hand appliqué stitch, and into each doily. I wanted to capture that gentle feeling with the use of delicate, lacy embroideries.

After the embroideries for our quilt top were complete, and the top assembled, my husband noticed a spool of 4" wide, flat lace that had been on the shelf in our studio, unused for many years. His suggestion of incorporating it into the border gave the graceful look that was the perfect finishing touch.

Embellishments are a true expression of our feelings for bits and pieces of our lives and creativity that have been put aside on a shelf or in a corner far too long. Bring them out, and use them, and you will be amazed at the results!

The vest pictured in this project chapter, embellished with lace and embroideries, was designed and made by our wonderful Viking educator, Bonnie Colonna. Bringing the design into her digitizing program, Stitch Editor Plus, she was able to break the design elements apart and use them strategically to enhance the denim vest.

The quilt was designed in remembrance of Britt's mother. Thank you for the inspiration Britt. May it give other quilters the warmth that I found in your creativity.

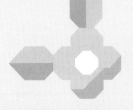

27

Quilt finishes to: 63 1/2" x 99 1/2"
Blocks A, B, and C finish to 18" squares.

MATERIALS

For Embroideries:
Robison Anton #40 weight rayon embroidery thread:
#2342 Natural white:

☐	Fabric I (pale yellow print)	Need 79 1/8"	2 3/8 yards
◼	Fabric II (medium blue print)	Need 78 1/4"	2 3/8 yard
◼	Fabric III (solid medium blue)	Need 112"	3 1/4 yards
◻	Fabric IV (light blue print)	Need 47 3/4"	1 1/2 yards
◼	Fabric V (medium green print)	Need 44 1/2"	1 3/8 yard
☐	Fabric VI (white on white print)	Need 5 1/2"	1/4 yard

1/4" wide bias. See our instructions for "quick bias trick"		6 1/2 yards
4" wide flat ecru lace		9 1/2 yards
Backing		6 yards

Techniques used:
Diagonal corners.

GREAT BEGINNER
PROJECT!

All "Q" units in cutting instructions stand for "quilt top." These are units that are not incorporated into the specific blocks, but are on the quilt top.

CUTTING

Cutting instructions shown in red indicate that the quantity of units is combined and cut in 2 or more places to conserve fabric.

From Fabric I, cut: (pale yellow print)
- One 9" wide strip. From this, cut:
  * Seven – 5 1/4" x 9" (A13)
  * Thirty-five – 1 1/8" sq. (A2a, A11a)
- Three 7 1/8" wide strips. From these, cut:
  * Twenty-eight – 3 1/2" x 7 1/8" (A9)
- One 6 1/2" wide strip. From this, cut:
  * Four – 6 1/2" sq. (B1)
  * Seventy-nine – 1 1/8" sq. (add to A2a, A11a)
- One 5 1/4" wide strip. From this, cut:
  * Fourteen – 2 3/8" x 5 1/4" (A4)
  * Thirty-five – 1 1/8" sq. (add to A2a, A11a)
- Two 4 3/8" wide strips. From these, cut:
  * Twenty-eight – 1 7/8" x 4 3/8" (A5)
  * Seventy-five – 1 1/8" sq. (add to A2a, A11a)
- One 4 1/8" wide strip. From this, cut:
  * Twenty-eight – 1" x 4 1/8" (A8)
  * Sixteen – 1 5/8" sq. (A6a, A7a)
- Three 1 7/8" wide strips. From these, cut:
  * Fifty-six – 1 7/8" sq. (A6b, A6c)
  * Twelve – 1 5/8" sq. (add to A6a, A7a)
- Five 1 3/4" wide strips. From these, cut:
  * 112 – 1 3/4" sq. (A3, A12)
  * Eight – 1 5/8" sq. (add to A6a, A7a)
- Six 1 5/8" wide strips. From these, cut:
  * 132 – 1 5/8" sq. (add to A6a, A7a)

From Fabric II, cut: (medium blue print)
- Ten 5" wide strips. From these, cut:
  * Two – 5" x 42" (side borders)
  * Four – 5" x 29 1/2" (side borders) Piece two 29 1/2" strips on opposite sides of one 42" wide strip. Make two to = 100" lengths.
  * Four – 5" x 32 1/4" (top & bottom borders) Piece two together to = two 64" lengths.
- From scrap, cut:
  * Fifty-six – 1 1/4" squares (A10a)
- Three 2 3/4" wide strips. From these and scrap, cut:
  * Fifty-six – 1 3/4" x 2 3/4" (A11)
- Eight 2 1/2" wide strips for straight-grain binding.

From Fabric III, cut: (solid medium blue)
- Seven 16" wide strips. From these, cut:
  * Twenty – 12" x 16" (B3, C1 for embroidery) Center completed embroidery and cut down to 6 1/2" squares.
  * Fifty-six – 1 3/4" x 2 3/4" (A2)
  * Fifty-six – 1 1/4" squares (A1a)

From Fabric IV, cut: (light blue print)
- One 20" wide strip. From this, cut:
  * 5/8" wide bias strips for wreath to = 6 1/2 yards.
- Three 6 1/2" wide strips. From these, cut:
  * Sixteen – 6 1/2" sq. (C3)
- Two 4 1/8" wide strips. From these, cut:
  * Twenty-eight – 2 3/4" x 4 1/8" (A7)

From Fabric V, cut: (medium green print)
- Six 6 1/2" wide strips. From these, cut:
  * Thirty-two – 6 1/2" sq. (B2, C2)
  * Twelve – 2 3/4" x 4 3/8" (A6)
- Two 2 3/4" wide strips. From these, cut:
  * Sixteen – 2 3/4" x 4 3/8" (add to A6)

From Fabric VI, cut: (white on white print)
- Two 2 3/4" wide strips. From these, cut:
  * Twenty-eight – 2 3/4" sq. (A1, A10)

ASSEMBLY

Making Block A

1. Use diagonal corner technique to make eight each of units 2 and 11. Use this technique to make four each of units 6 and 7, and two each of units 1 and 10.

2. To assemble the block, begin by assembling Section A first. Join

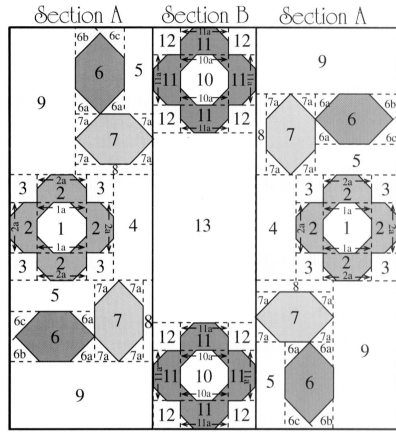

Block A. Make 7. Finishes to 18" square.

flower units 2-1-2 in a row . Join units 3-2-3 in two rows as shown. Join the three rows together; then add Unit 4 to side as illustrated.

3. Join units 5 and 6. Join units 7 and 8. Join these two combined leaf units together; then add Unit 9 as shown. Referring to diagram above, join the three parts of Section A together, checking to make sure they are in the correct position. Make two of Section A.

4. For Section B, make the flowers first. Begin by joining units 11-10-11. Join units 12-11-12. Join the three small rows together to form the flower. Make two. Join the flowers to opposite short ends of Unit 13 to complete Section B.

5. Join the three sections of Block A together. Make 7 of Block A.

Making Block B.

1. If you are stitching embroideries, your 6 1/2" squares will be cut for this block and for Block C. If you do not have an embroidery machine, both blocks B and C make nice 9-Patch blocks.

2. To assemble the block, begin by joining squares 3-2-3 in a row as shown. Press seams towards square 2. Make two of these rows. For center row, join squares 2-1-2 and press seams towards square 2. Join the three rows, interlocking seams to match them.

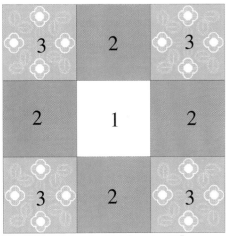

Block B. Make 4. Finishes to 18" square.

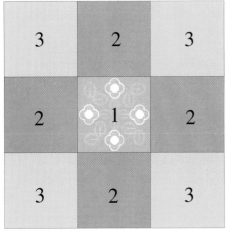

Block C. Make 4. Finishes to 18" square.

Making Block C.

1. To assemble Block C, begin by joining squares 3-2-3 in a row as shown. Press the seams towards square 2. Make two of these rows. For center row, join squares 2-1-2 and press seams towards square 2. Join the three rows, interlocking seams to match them.

Making Block A Wreath

1. Refer to the instructions in the floral frame at the bottom of the page for making your own press on bias. You will need a total of approximately 6 1/2 yards. We pressed the bias on; then ran a wide zig zag stitch at each short end, and top stitched the bias in place.

Making The Quilt Top

1. Refer to diagram of finished quilt on page 31. To assemble the quilt top, begin at the top and join Block B, Block A, and Block B in a horizontal row. For second row, join Blocks A, C, and A in a row. For third row, join Blocks C, A, and C in a row. Repeat Row two for fourth row, and repeat Row 1 for fifth row. Join the rows together matching all corner seams.

Making The Borders

1. Place lace along one long edge of each border. Baste in place.
2. Find the center of top and bottom quilt edges, and top and bottom lace borders. Pin centers. Join top and bottom borders, beginning and ending 1/4" from edge of the quilt top, and backstitch to stabilize. Repeat for side borders. Please note that borders will extend beyond ends of quilt to allow for mitering the corners.
3. To miter corners, refer to diagram at top of the page. Lace will be mitered into the corner seam. Trim the seam after mitering the corner.

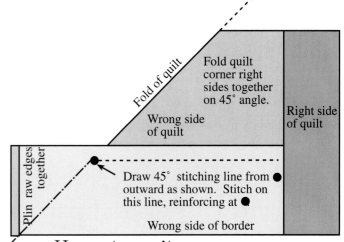

How to miter a corner.

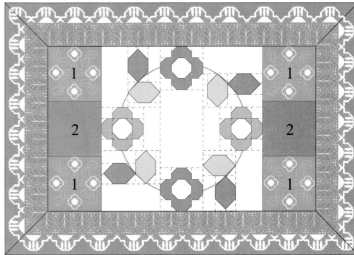

Pillow sham. Finishes to 18" x 30" plus 5" flange

MATERIALS FOR SHAM

	Fabric I (pale yellow print)	Need 11 3/4"	1/2 yard
	Fabric II (medium blue print)	Need 70"	2 1/8 yards
	Fabric III (solid medium blue)	Need 32"	1 yard
	Fabric IV (light blue print)	Need 2 3/4"	1/8 yard
	Fabric V (medium green print)	Need 6 1/2"	1/4 yard
	Fabric VI (white on white print)	Need 2 3/4"	1/8 yard
	Backing		1 1/2 yards
	4" wide flat lace		4 yards

Quick Bias Trick For Rose Of Sharon Wreath Block:

To make your own press on bias to match the green fabric used in your quilt, use Clover's "Bias Maker" for 1/4" wide bias. Follow instructions on package. We cut the bias strips a very scant 3/4" wide. Next we cut strips of Steam A Seam 2™ that were approximately 3/16" wide.

After the bias is pressed, follow package instructions on how to use Steam A Seam 2™, and press the Steam A Seam 2 strips onto the back of the bias strips. Remove the paper from the back of the Steam-A-Seam 2. You have now made your own "press on bias."

From Fabric III, cut: (solid medium blue)
- Two 16" wide strips. From these, cut:
  - Four – 12" x 16 ". (Q1 for embroidery) After embroidery is completed, center and cut down to 6 1/2" sq.
  - Eight – 1 3/4" x 2 3/4" (A2)
  - Eight – 1 1/4" squares (A1a)

From Fabric IV, cut: (light blue print)
- One 2 3/4" wide strip. From this, cut:
  - Four – 2 3/4" x 4 1/8" (A7)

From Fabric V, cut: (medium green print)
- One 6 1/2" wide strip. From this, cut:
  - Two – 6 1/2" sq. (Q2)
  - Four – 2 3/4" x 4 3/8" (A6)
- Cut 5/8" wide bias strips for wreath from remainder of 20" wide strip for quilt.

From Fabric VI, cut: (white on white print)
- One 2 3/4" wide strip. From this, cut:
  - Four – 2 3/4" sq. (A1, A10)

SHAM ASSEMBLY

1. Refer to instructions for Making Block A on page 29. Make one of Block A, and use any large scraps of bias for the wreath.
2. Join embroidered 6 1/2" squares of Fabric III with 6 1/2" squares of Fabric V. Join in vertical row as shown. Make 2. Add to opposite sides of Block A.
3. Refer to Making The Border instructions for quilt, and add mitered borders with lace.
4. Press under 1/4" twice on one 28" side of each sham backing piece. Top stitch in place. Place the two sham backs face down on sham front, overlapping hemmed edges, and pin. Use 1/4" seam and stitch around outer edge of sham. Turn right side out, press.
5. After pressing top, pin, along flange seam lines and top stitch with coordinating thread through all thicknesses.

FOR PILLOW

1. Refer to quilt directions and make one of Block C. For flange, cut four 5" x 28" pieces of Fabric II and lace. Cut two 17 1/2" x 28" pieces of Fabric II for pillow backing.
2. Refer to quilt instructions for adding the borders and mitering the corners. Press under 1/4" twice on one 17 1/2" side of each pillow backing piece. Top stitch in place. Place the two pillow backs face down on pillow front, overlapping hemmed edges, and pin. Use 1/4" seam and stitch around outer edge of pillow. Turn right side out and press.
3. After pressing top, pin, along flange seam lines and top stitch with coordinating thread through all thicknesses.

Finished quilt diagram.

CUTTING FOR SHAM

From Fabric I, cut: (pale yellow print)
- One 9" wide strip. From this, cut:
  - One – 5 1/4" x 9" (A13)
  - Four – 3 1/2" x 7 1/8" (A9)
  - Two – 2 3/8" x 5 1/4" (A4)
  - Four – 1 7/8" x 4 3/8" (A5)
- From remainder of the 1 7/8" cuts above, cut:
  - Eight – 1 7/8" squares (A6b, A6c)
  - Four – 1" x 4 1/8" (A8)
  - Sixteen – 1 3/4" sq. (A3, A12)
- One 1 5/8" wide strip. From this, cut:
  - Twenty-four – 1 5/8" sq. (A6a, A7a)
- One 1 1/8" wide strip. From this, cut:
  - Thirty-two – 1 1/8" sq. (A2a, A11a)

From Fabric II, cut: (medium blue print)
- Two 24" wide strips. From these, cut:
  - Two – 24" x 28" (backing)
- Four 5 1/2" wide strips. From these, cut:
  - Two – 5 1/2" x 40" (top & bottom borders)
  - Two – 5 1/2" x 28" (side borders)
  - Eight – 1 3/4" x 2 3/4" (A11)
  - Eight – 1 1/4" sq. (A10a)

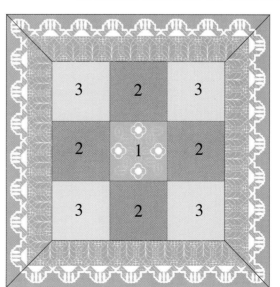

Pillow. Finishes to 18" plus 5" flange.

Rose of Sharon Table Runner

Although our table runner is presented in a holiday theme, country reds, greens and golds are appropriate for any time of the year.

Designed with a beginner in mind, utilizing one simple "quick piecing" technique, it will catch the eye of the most experienced quilter for its elegance. Embroideries add to its charm, but may be substituted with a circular quilting design.

Warm, inviting candles and colorful glassware are an invitation for everyone to join around the table no matter what the occasion.

Table runner finishes to: 22" x 60"
Block A finishes to 18" square.

MATERIALS

☐	Fabric I (ivory print)	Need 44 5/8"	1 3/8 yards
■	Fabric II (brick red print)	Need 17 1/4"	5/8 yard
■	Fabric III (dark red print)	Need 4"	1/4 yard
■	Fabric IV (light olive print)	Need 9 3/8"	3/8 yard
■	Fabric V (dark olive print)	Need 24 1/8"	3/4 yard
☐	Fabric VI (gold print)	Need 19 3/4"	5/8 yard
	Backing		2 yards

3 yards. 1/4" wide bias. Read our instructions for making your own press on bias given in Rose Of Sharon quilt instructions.

Techniques used:
Diagonal Corners

GREAT FOR A BEGINNER!

Instructions for making reversible napkins may be found on page 16. Napkin folds are shown on page 34.

For Embroideries:
Robison Anton #40 weight rayon embroidery thread: #2282 Flite Green (lt. green), #2252 Russet (burgundy), and #2606 TH Gold.

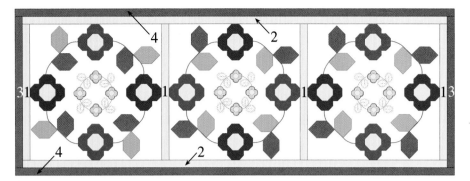

• Six 1 1/2" wide strips. From these, cut:
  * Four – 1 1/2" x 29 1/2" (Q2) Piece two together to make two 58 1/2" lengths.
  * Four – 1 1/2" x 18 1/2" (Q1)

ASSEMBLY

Making Block A

1. To make Block A for the table runner, refer to "Making Block A" on page 29. Make 3 of Block A. Embroideries are stitched after the block has been completed. Find block center, and center

CUTTING

From Fabric I, cut: (ivory print)
• One 16" wide strip. From this, cut:
  * Two – 16" sq. (napkins)
  * Three – 5 1/4" x 9" (A13) Place horizontally.
• One 7 1/8" wide strip. From this, cut:
  * Twelve – 3 1/2" x 7 1/8" (A9)
• One 5 1/4" wide strip. From this, cut:
  * Six – 2 3/8" x 5 1/4" (A4)
  * Twelve – 1 7/8" x 4 3/8" (A5)
• One 4 1/8" wide strip. From this, cut:
  * Twelve – 1" x 4 1/8" (A8)
  * Seventy-eight – 1 1/8" sq. (A2a, A11a)
• Two 1 7/8" wide strips. From these, cut:
  * Twenty-four – 1 7/8" sq. (A6b, A6c)
  * Eighteen – 1 1/8" sq. (add to A2a, A11a)
• Two 1 3/4" wide strips. From these, cut:
  * Forty-eight – 1 3/4" sq. (A3, A12)
• Three 1 5/8" wide strips. From these, cut:
  * Seventy-two – 1 5/8" sq. (A6a, A7a)

From Fabric II, cut: (brick red print)
• One 16" wide print. From this, cut:
  * Two – 16" squares (napkins)
  * Twenty-four – 1 3/4" x 2 3/4" (A2)
• One 1 1/4" wide strip. From this, cut:
  * Twenty-four – 1 1/4" sq. (A1a)

From Fabric III, cut: (dark red print)
• One 2 3/4" wide strip. From this, cut:
  * Twenty-four – 1 3/4" x 2 3/4" (A11)
• One 1 1/4" wide strip. From this, cut:
  * Twenty-four – 1 1/4" sq. (A10a)

From Fabric IV, cut: (light olive print)
• One 4 3/8" wide strip. From this, cut:
  * Twelve – 2 3/4" x 4 3/8" (A6)
• Two 2 1/2" wide strips. From these, cut:
  * Four – 2 1/2" x 12" (napkin rings)

From Fabric V, cut: (dark olive print)
• One 4 1/8" wide strip. From this, cut:
  * Twelve – 2 3/4" x 4 1/8" (A7)
• Five 2 1/2" wide strips for straight-grain binding.
• Five 1 1/2" wide strips. From these, cut:
  * Four – 1 1/2" x 30 1/2" (Q4) Piece two together to make two 60 1/2" lengths.
  * Two – 1 1/2" x 20 1/2" (Q3)

From Fabric VI, cut: (gold print)
• One 2 3/4" wide strip. From this, cut:
  * Twelve – 2 3/4" sq. (A1, A10)
• Four 2" wide strips for napkin binding.

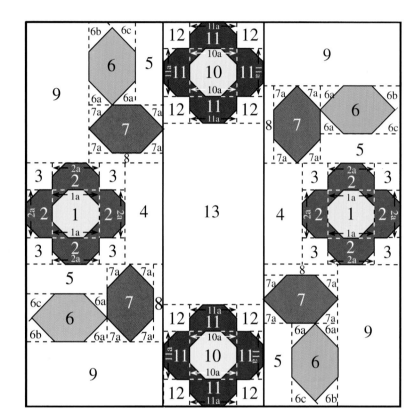

of embroidery. Stitch embroidery. Read instructions for making your own press on bias on page 30, and complete your wreath as directed on that page.

Completing The Table Runner

1. Refer to illustration above. Join blocks together with Unit Q1 between blocks and at the ends of row as shown. Join previously pieced Unit Q2 to top and bottom. Join Unit Q3 to opposite short ends of table runner; then add Unit Q4 to top and bottom.

QUILTING AND FINISHING

Extra leaves were quilted around the wreath and the patchwork was ditched. We used 180" of straight-grain binding to bind the edge.

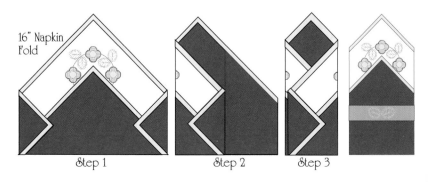

16" Napkin Fold

Step 1   Step 2   Step 3

Over the years, Robert and I have made many quilts, some of which are special favorites. Most of the quilts that we make are used for photography, and then for shows and other special events. It is seldom that one is actually used for our bed. While vacationing in northern Idaho this past summer, we found a lovely Alder bed. When this design was first drafted, we knew where it belonged. Our photographer captured the warm, luxurious feeling we felt when the quilt was first placed on our new bed with crochet accessories.

Hearts & Flowers

Quilt finishes to: 96" x 111"
Block A finishes to 18" square.
Blocks B and C finish to 6" squares.

MATERIALS

☐	Fabric I (pale tan print)	Need 167 1/4" / 4 7/8 yards
■	Fabric II (navy print)	Need 180" / 5 1/4 yards
▨	Fabric III (light blue print)	Need 17" / 5/8 yard
▨	Fabric IV (medium blue check)	Need 49 1/2" / 1 1/2 yards
▨	Fabric V (tan check)	Need 42 3/4" / 1 3/8 yards
▨	Fabric VI (honey brown print)	Need 38 1/4" / 1 1/4 yards
■	Fabric VII (medium rust print)	Need 83 3/4" / 2 1/2 yards
	Backing	8 5/8 yards

CUTTING

All "Q" units in cutting instructions stand for "quilt top." These are units that are not incorporated into the specific blocks, but are on the quilt top.

Cutting instructions shown in red indicate that the quantity of units is combined and cut in 2 or more different places to conserve fabric.

☐ **From Fabric I, cut:** (pale tan print)
• One 6 1/2" wide strip. From this, cut:
   * Four – 6 1/2" sq. (Q3)
   * Ninety-six – 1" sq. (A2a, B1a)
• Three 4 3/4" wide strips. From these, cut:
   * Sixty – 2" x 4 3/4" (A16)
• Three 3 1/4" wide strips. From these, cut:
   * Sixty – 2" x 3 1/4" (A15)
• Twenty 2 3/4" wide strips. From these, cut:
   * 240 – 2 3/4" sq. (A5a, A9a, A11a)
   * Eighty – 2" x 2 3/4" (A7)
• Eighteen 2 1/2" wide strips. From these, cut:
   * 109 – 2 1/2" sq. (A6a, C1)
   * 196 – 1 3/4" x 2 1/2" (A3, B2)
   * Sixty – 1 1/2" x 2 1/2" (A13a)
• Seven 1 3/4" wide strips. From these, cut:

Techniques used:
Diagonal Corners and
Diagonal Ends with some
"quick piecing" tricks!

* 160 – 1 3/4" sq. (A4a)
* Thirteen 1 1/2" wide strips. From these, cut:
  * 360 – 1 1/2" sq. (A9b, A10a, A13c, A14a)
* Five 1" wide strips. From these, cut:
  * 180 – 1" sq. (add to A2a, B1a)

 From Fabric II, cut: (navy print)
* One 4 3/4" wide strip. From this, cut:
  * Twenty – 2" x 4 3/4" (A20)
* Nineteen 3 1/2" wide strips. From these, cut:
  * Five – 3 1/2" x 42" (Q1, Q4, Q5)
  * Four – 3 1/2" x 39 1/2" (Q2) Join two together to = two 78 1/2" long strips.
  * Four – 3 1/2" x 33 3/4" (Q4) Join two to opposite short ends of one 42" long strip to = two 108 1/2" long strips.
  * Two – 3 1/2" x 27 3/4" (Q5) Join two to opposite short ends of one 42" long strip to = two 96 1/2" long strips.
  * Four – 3 1/2" x 24 3/4" (Q1) Join two to opposite short ends of one 42" long strip to = two 90 1/2" long strips.
  * Eighty – 3" x 3 1/2" (A9, A11)
  * Twenty – 1 1/2" x 3 1/2" (A17)
* One 3 1/4" wide strip. From this, cut:
  * Twenty – 2" x 3 1/4" (A19)
* Four 2 3/4" wide strips. From these, cut:
  * Eighty – 2" x 2 3/4" (A7a)
* Twenty-four 2 1/2" wide strips. Eleven for straight-grain binding. From remaining thirteen strips, cut:
  * Eighty – 2 1/2" sq. (A6b)
  * Sixty – 1 1/2" x 2 1/2" (A13)
  * 232 – 1 1/4" x 2 1/2" (B3, C3)
* Four 1 1/2" wide strips. From these, cut:
  * 100 – 1 1/2" sq. (A12a, A17b, A18a)
* Fourteen 1 1/4" wide strips. From these & scrap, cut:
  * 464 – 1 1/4" sq. (B4a, C4a)
* Eleven 1" wide strips. From these and scrap, cut:
  * 464 – 1" sq. (B2a, C2a)

 From Fabric III, cut: (light blue print)
* Six 2 1/2" wide strips. From these, cut:
  * Twenty-nine – 2 1/2" sq. (B1)
  * Eighty – 2" x 2 1/2" (A2)
* Two 1" wide strips. From these, cut:
  * Eighty – 1" sq. (A1a)

 From Fabric IV, cut: (medium blue check)
* Eleven 4 1/2" wide strips. From these, cut:
  * 160 – 2 3/4" x 4 1/2" (A5)

 From Fabric V, cut: (tan check)
* Seven 3 1/4" wide strips. From these, cut:
  * Eighty – 3 1/4" sq. (A4)
* Eight 2 1/2" wide strips. From these and scrap, cut:
  * 116 – 2 1/2" sq. (B4)

 From Fabric VI, cut: (honey brown print)
* Seven 3 1/4" wide strips. From these, cut:
  * Eighty – 3 1/4" sq. (A14, A18)
* Five 2 1/2" wide strips. From these, cut:
  * 116 – 1 3/4" x 2 1/2" (C2)
* Three 1" wide strips. From these, cut:
  * 116 – 1" sq. (C1a)

 From Fabric VII, cut: (med. rust print)
* Twenty 2 3/4" wide strips. From these, cut:
  * Eighty – 2 3/4" x 3" (A10, A12)
  * Eighty – 2" x 2 3/4" (A8)
  * 160 – 1 3/4" x 2 3/4" (A6)

* Eighty – 1 1/2" x 2 3/4" (A13b, A17a)
* Nine 2 1/2" wide strips. From these, cut:
  * 136 – 2 1/2" sq. (A1, C4)
* Five 1 1/4" wide strips. From these, cut:
  * 160 – 1 1/4" sq. (A5b)

ASSEMBLY

Making Block A

1. Use diagonal corner technique to make eight of Unit 5 (see diagrams for making the combined heart section), four each of units 2, and 4. Use this technique to make three each of units 9, 10, and 14; then one each of units 1, 11, 12, and 18.

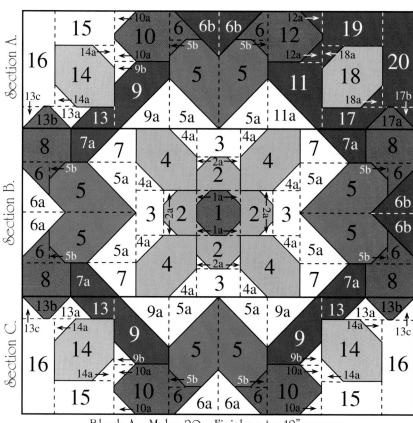

Block A. Make 20. Finishes to 18" square.

2. Use diagonal end technique to make four mirror image Unit 7, and three of mirror image Unit 13. Use this technique to make one of Unit 17. Refer to illustrations of these units for easier assembly.

3. To make the combined heart (5-6 units), refer to diagram below, and begin by using diagonal corner technique to make eight of Unit 5, checking placement of mirror image diagonal corners. Join Unit 6 to top of each heart section. Join diagonal corner Unit 6a as shown. Trim seam and press. Join the two mirror image heart sections together, matching seams. Be sure to take note that two of the large diagonal corner units are 6a from Fabric I, and two are 6b from Fabric II.

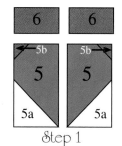
Step 1

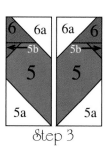
Step 2

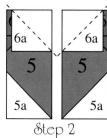
Step 3

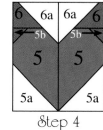
Step 4

4. The diagram at right shows you how to make mirror image Unit 7. Refer to this illustration for correct diagonal slant.

5. The diagram below shows you how to assemble mirror image Unit 13. This is a continuous diagonal end that is shown in our "technique" section. Follow the illustrations and refer to

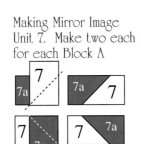

Making Mirror Image Unit 7. Make two each for each Block A

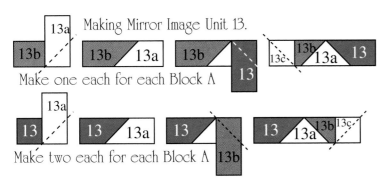

Making Mirror Image Unit 13.
Make one each for each Block A

Make two each for each Block A

Block A drawing for correct positioning of this unit as three of them will be made for the block. Add diagonal corners after diagonal ends are complete.

Refer to diagram at right and make one of Unit 17 as shown.

Making Unit 17

6. Block A is divided into three sections. Refer to illustration of the block. Begin assembly with Section A. Starting with units to the left of the heart, join units 9 and 10. Join units 14 and 15; then add Unit 16 to left side as shown. Add Unit 13 to bottom of combined units 14-16. Join combined units 9-10 to combined units 13-16; then add to left side of heart, matching seams.

7. For units to the right of heart, join units 11 and 12. Join units 18 and 19; then add Unit 20 to right side of these combined units. Add Unit 17 to bottom of combined units. Join the 11-12 units to left side of combined units 17-20; then join all of these combined units to the right of the heart to complete Section A.

8. For Section B, begin by joining units 3-2-1-2-3 in a vertical row as shown. Join units 2 and 3. Make two. Join units 4 to top an bottom of combined 2-3 units. Join to opposite sides of combined 1-3 center units to complete the center flower. Join mirror image Unit 7 and Unit 8 as shown, checking block diagram for correct placement of Unit 7 mirror image. Join these combined units to opposite sides of heart. Make two and join to opposite sides of center flower to complete Section B.

9. For Section C, units 9-16 (on both sides of heart) are joined in the same manner, although checking for correct placement is essential as they are mirror images.

10. For Section C, refer to Step 5 for instructions on assembling units 9-16, keeping in mind the correct placement for mirror image units.

11. Join the three sections together, matching seams to complete Block A. Make 20. Your unfinished block should measure 18 1/2" square.

Making Blocks B and C

1. For each block: Use diagonal corner technique to make four each of units 2 and 4, and one of Unit 1. Refer to Step 8 for assembly of flower block. Your unfinished block will measure 6 1/2" square. The flower blocks are perfect for chain piecing.

Quilt Assembly

1. Refer to large drawing of complete quilt on page 40. You will join five rows of four A blocks per row. When joining the blocks, be sure that seams match, and check illustration frequently for correct placement of corner colors.

2. When all of the blocks have been joined for the top, add previously pieced border Q1 to opposite sides of quilt. Press seams towards border. Join pieced border Q2 to top and bottom of quilt top.

3. The floral border on this quilt is so striking when completed, that it is more than just a "finishing touch." In joining the B and C blocks together to make the border, it is important to check the illustration frequently as the blocks are alternated all the way around the quilt. Begin with the top and bottom borders. There are 13 flowers in each row. The top border begins and ends with Block B, and the bottom border begins and ends with Block C. Join the blocks together matching leaf seams; then add them to top and bottom of quilt, finding the center of the quilt and the center of the border. Pin the centers and stitch in place.

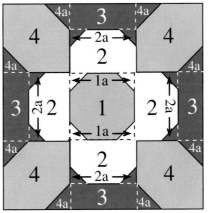

Block B. Finishes to 6" sq.
Make 29 for quilt.
Make 2 for pillowcases
Make 4 for pillow.

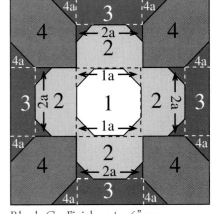

Block C. Finishes to 6" sq.
Make 29 for quilt.
Make 4 for pillowcases.
Make 5 for pillow.

4. Both side floral borders are the same, with 16 flowers in each row. Join Q3 units to opposite short ends of the floral side borders. Join the borders to quilt sides as in Step 3, checking diagram for proper placement.

5. Join pieced border Q4 to sides of quilt; then add border Q5 to bottom of quilt to complete the top.

Quilt Finishes to 96" x 111"

QUILTING AND FINISHING

Faye "ditched" the patchwork and quilted small flowers in spaces on the quilt top. She added a feathered border in medium blue thread to complete the quilting. We used approximately 425" of straight-grain French fold binding.

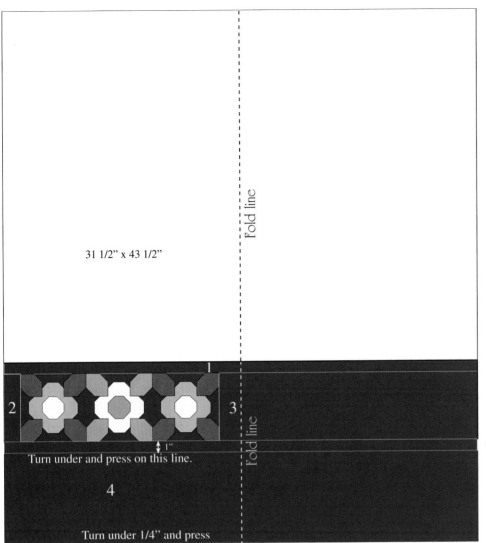

31 1/2" x 43 1/2"

Fold line

1

2

3

Fold line

↕ 1"

Turn under and press on this line.

4

Turn under 1/4" and press

Pillowcase. Finishes to 21 1/2" x 39"

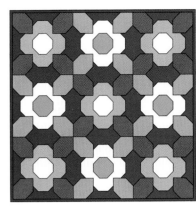

Pillow finishes to 18" square.

- Two 6 1/2" wide strips. From these, cut:
  * Two – 6 1/2" x 24" (Q3)
  * Two – 2" x 6 1/2" (Q2)
- Cut remainder into eight 1 1/4" wide strips. From these, cut:
  * Twenty-four – 1 1/4" x 2 1/2" (B3, C3)
  * Forty-eight – 1 1/4" sq. (B4a, C4a)
- From scrap, cut:
  * Thirty-six – 1" sq. (B2a, C2a)
- Two 1 1/2" wide strips. From these, cut:
  * Two – 1 1/2" x 43 1/2" (Q1)
- One 1" wide strip. From this, cut:
  * Twelve – 1" sq. (add to B2a, C2a)

From Fabric III, cut: (lt. blue print)
- Two – 2 1/2" sq. (B1)

From Fabric IV, cut: (tan check)
- One 2 1/2" wide strip. From this, cut:
  * Eight – 2 1/2" sq. (B4)

From Fabric V, cut: (honey brown print)
- One 1 3/4" wide strip. From this, cut:
  * Sixteen – 1 3/4" x 2 1/2" (C2)
- One 1" wide strip. From this, cut:
  * Sixteen – 1" sq. (C1a)

From Fabric VI, cut: (medium rust print)
- One 2 1/2" strip. From this, cut:
  * Eight – 2 1/2" sq. (C4)

MAKING THE PILLOWCASES

MATERIALS

☐	Fabric I (pale tan print)	Need 65 1/2" 1 3/4 yards
■	Fabric II (navy print)	Need 36" 1 1/8 yards
▦	Fabric III (lt. blue print)	Need 3" x 6" Scrap
▦	Fabric IV (tan check)	Need 2 1/2" 1/8 yard
▦	Fabric V (honey brown pt.)	Need 2 3/4" 1/8 yard
▦	Fabric VI (med. rust print)	Need 2 1/2" 1/8 yard

CUTTING

From Fabric I, cut: (pale tan print)
- Two 31 1/2" wide strips. From these, cut:
  * Two – 31 1/2" x 43 1/2" (pillow case)
- One 2 1/2" wide strip. From this, cut:
  * Four – 2 1/2" sq. (C1)
  * Eight – 1 3/4" x 2 1/2" (B2)
  * Eight – 1" sq. (B1a)

From Fabric II, cut: (navy print)
- Two 9 1/2" wide strips. From these, cut:
  7* Two – 9 1/2" x 43 1/2" (Q4)

Making The Pillowcases

1. Refer to illustrations and instructions for Blocks B and C on page 39. Make one of Block B and two of Block C for each pillowcase. Join in a horizontal row as shown.

2. To assemble, refer to pillowcase diagram above and begin by joining Unit Q2 to left side of flowers and Unit Q3 to right side. Add Unit Q1 to top and Unit Q4 to bottom.

3. Fold the pillowcase in half, right sides together, and serge or use overcast stitch around 2 sides, leaving bottom open. Turn right side out and press under 1/4" hem. Press the lining up inside, about 1" below the floral border. Turn pillowcase wrong side out, and whip stitch the lining in place. Lining should cover raw seams of border.

For The Pillow:

1. Refer to page 39 to review instructions for blocks B & C. Make four of Block B and five of Block C. Join together in rows as shown.

2. For pillow backing, cut two 12 1/2" x 18 1/2". Press under 1/4" twice on one 18 1/2" side of each pillow backing piece. Top stitch in place. Place the two pillow backs face down on pillow front, overlapping hemmed edges, and pin. Use 1/4" seam and stitch around outer edge of pillow. Turn right side out and press.

41

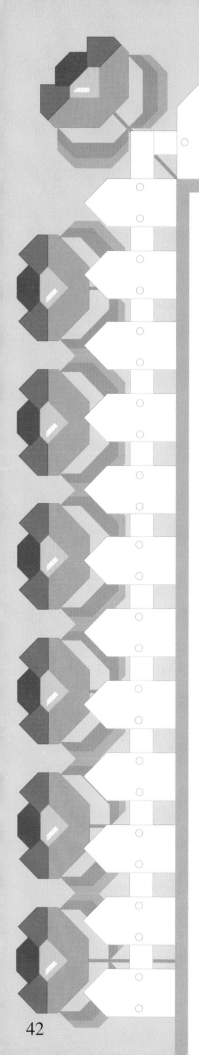

Baltimore Violet Quilt

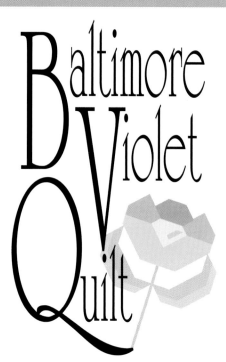

As wild violets have always been a favorite of mine, and African Violets were on every window sill in the home where I grew up, my imagination went wild with this ensemble of designs.

It gave all of us the opportunity to show how many different faces there are to one motif.

From bedroom or sun porch, to kitchen and dining area, this happy little grouping of violets can be used in many ways. So turn your own imagination loose, and add the accessories of your choice.

Quilt finishes to: 74" square
Blocks A and B finish to 7" square.
Block C finishes to 2" X 4"

> **Techniques used:**
> Diagonal Corners, Diagonal Ends.,
> and Strip Sets

MATERIALS

☐	Fabric I (white on ivory print)	Need 82 1/4"	2 1/2 yards
☐	Fabric II (white on white print)	Need 43 1/2"	1 3/8 yards
☐	Fabric III (light green print)	Need 39 1/2"	1 1/4 yards
☐	Fabric IV (medium green print)	Need 19 1/4"	5/8 yard
☐	Fabric V (dark green print)	Need 18"	5/8 yard
☐	Fabric VI (light violet print)	Need 12 3/8"	1/2 yard
☐	Fabric VII (dark violet print)	Need 42"	1 1/4 yards
☐	Fabric VIII (light yellow print)	Need 4 1/4"	1/4 yard
	1/4" wide press on dark green bias by Clover.		3 1/8 yards.
	Backing		4 1/2 yards

For Embroideries:

Robison Anton #40 wt. rayon embroidery thread: #2424 Cachet (med. violet), #2276 Lavender (lt. Violet), #2410 Lt. Kelly (med. green), #2211 Nile (lt. Green), #2493 Light Bronze and #3606 TH Gold

CUTTING

From Fabric I, cut: (white on ivory print)
- One 31 1/2"x 42" strip. From this, cut:
  * One – 31 1/2" square (Q1 for embroidery). When embroidery is complete, center and cut down to 28 1/2" square.
- From remainder, cut:
  * Four – 2 1/2" x 30 1/2" (Q8) Piece two together to make two 60 1/2" lengths.
- Four 2 1/2" x 42" strips. From these, cut:
  * Four – 2 1/2" x 28 1/2" (Q7) Piece two together to make two 56 1/2" lengths.
  * Four – 2 1/2" sq. (B12)
  * Eight – 1 3/4" x 2 1/2" (B8)
  * Eight – 1 1/4" x 2 3/4" (B10)
  * Four – 2 3/8" sq. (B1)
  * Four – 1 7/8" sq. (B7a)
- Five 2" wide strips. From these, cut:
  * Ninety-six – 2" sq. (A5a, A9b)

* Eight – 1 3/8" x 1 1/2" (B2)
- Four 1 3/4" wide strips. From these and scrap, cut:
  * Fifty-six – 1 3/4" sq. (A9a, B4b)
  * Twenty-four – 1 3/4" x 3" (A7)
- Thirteen 1 1/2" wide strips. From these, cut:
  * Twenty-four – 1 1/2" x 7 1/2" (A10)
  * Forty-eight – 1 1/2" x 4" (A6)
  * Ninety-six – 1 1/2" sq. (A4a, A8a)
- One 1 1/4" wide strip. From this, cut:
  * Thirty-two – 1 1/4" sq. (B9a)
- Three 1" x 42" strips. From these, cut:
  * Ninety-six – 1" sq. (A1a, A4b)

From Fabric II, cut: (white on white print)
- Eight 4 1/2" wide strips. From these, cut:
  * 128 – 2 1/2" x 4 1/2" (C1)
- Five 1 1/2" wide strips for Strip Set 1

From Fabric III, cut: (light green print)
- One 4 1/2" wide strip. From this, cut:
  * Eight – 4 1/2" sq. (Q4, Q11)

43

- Five 2 1/2" strips for Strip Set 1.
- Fifteen 1 1/2" wide strips. Five for Strip Set 1.

From remaining ten strips, cut:
- * 256 – 1 1/2" sq. (C1a)

 From Fabric IV, cut: (medium green print)
- Four 2 3/4" wide strips. From these, cut:
  - * Forty-eight – 2 3/4" sq. (A9)
  - * Eight – 1 3/4" x 2 3/4" (B11)
- Four 1 3/4" wide strips. From these, cut:
  - * Ninety-six – 1 1/2" x 1 3/4" (A6a, A8)
- One 1 1/4" wide strip. From this, cut:
  - * Sixteen – 1 1/4" x 2 1/2" (B9)

 From Fabric V, cut: (dark green print)
- Twelve 1 1/2" wide strips. From these, cut:
  - * Two – 1 1/2" x 42 1/2" (Q6)
  - * Two – 1 1/2" x 40 1/2" (Q5)
  - * Four – 1 1/2" x 31 1/2" (Q10) Piece two together to make two 62 1/2" lengths.
  - * Four – 1 1/2" x 30 1/2" (Q9) Piece two together to make two 60 1/2" lengths.

 From Fabric VI, cut: (light violet print)
- Three 2 1/2" wide strips. From these, cut:
  - * Forty-eight – 2" x 2 1/2" (A5)
  - * Twenty-one – 1 1/2" x 2 1/2" (A3)
- One 1 7/8" x 42" strip. From this, cut:
  - * Four – 1 7/8" x 3 5/8" (B7)
  - * Four – 1 7/8" x 2 1/4" (B6)
  - * Eight – 1 7/8" sq. (B4a)
- Two 1 1/2" wide strips. From these, cut:
  - * Forty-eight – 1 1/2" sq. (A2b)
  - * Three - 1 1/2" x 2 1/2" (add to A3)

 From Fabric VII, cut: (dark violet print)
- One 2 3/4" wide strip. From this, cut:
  - * Eight – 2 3/8" x 2 3/4" (B4)
  - * Forty-six – 1" sq. (A2a)
- Thirteen 2 1/2" wide strips. From these, cut:
  - * Four – 2 1/2" x 37 1/2" (Q13) Piece two together to make two 74 1/2" lengths.
  - * Four – 2 1/2" x 35 1/2" (Q12) Piece two together to make two 70 1/2" lengths.
  - * Two – 2 1/2" x 32 1/2" (Q3)
  - * Two – 2 1/2" x 28 1/2" (Q2)
  - * Twenty-four – 1 3/4" x 2 1/2" (A1)
  - * Sixteen – 1 3/8" sq. (B1a, B3, B5a)
- Three 2 1/4" wide strips. From these, cut:
  - * Forty-eight – 2" x 2 1/4" (A4)
  - * Two – 1" sq. (add to A2a)

 From Fabric VIII, cut: (light yellow print)
- One 2 1/4" wide strip. From this, cut:
  - * Four – 2 1/4" sq. (B5)
  - * Eight – 2" x 2 1/2" (A2)
- One 2" wide strip. From this, cut:
  - * Sixteen – 2" x 2 1/2" (add to A2)

All "Q" units in cutting instructions stand for "quilt top." These are units that are not incorporated into the specific blocks, but are on the quilt top.

* Please note that ←——→ shown on any unit indicates the longest side of the unit. We show this when difference of measurement (length and width) is only 1/8".

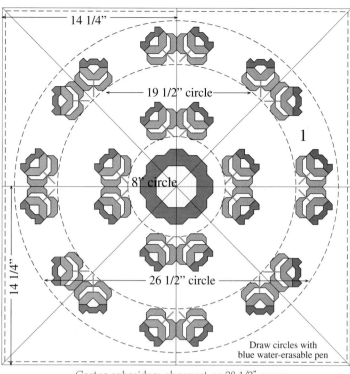

Draw circles with blue water-erasable pen

Center embroidery placement on 28 1/2" square

ASSEMBLY

The embroideries in this project are certainly more than an embellishment. They are the main characters, surrounded by a patchwork violet audience inside a charming picket fence.

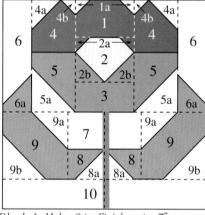

Block A. Make 24. Finishes to 7" square.

The diagram at the top of the page shows the exact placement for the embroideries. If this placement is followed, your embroidered center should be as stunning as the one that Bonnie stitched for us. We have suggested cutting a 31 1/2" square to allow more room for you to work with. This square will be cut down to 28 1/2" after the embroideries are completed.

Piecing Block A

1. Use diagonal corner technique to make two each of mirror image units 4, 5, 8, and 9. Make one of units 1 and 2.
2. Use diagonal end technique to make two of mirror image Unit 6. Correct stitching placement of this unit is illustrated below.
3. To assemble Block A, begin by joining units 1, 2, and 3 in a vertical row. Join units 4 and 5, referring to illustration for correct placement of mirror image units. Add combined 4-5 units to opposite sides of combined units 1-2-3; then add mirror image Unit 6 to opposite sides of violet as shown.
4. Join units 8 together as shown; then add Unit 7 across the top. Join mirror image Unit 9 to opposite sides of combined units 7-8; then add Unit 10 to bottom.
5. Before joining the flower and leaf sections together, cut twenty-four 3 3/4" long pieces of 1/4" wide press on bias. Pin the bias right side facing down in the center of Unit 3, with raw edge of bias and bottom edge

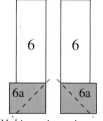

Making mirror image Unit 6 for Block A

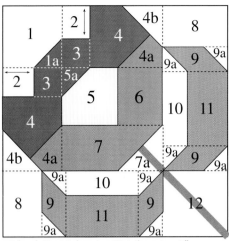

Block B. Make 4. Finishes to 7" square.

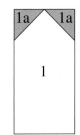

Block C - Make 128
Finishes to 2" x 4"

Quilt Assembly

1. After all blocks are completed and center embroidery area is cut to 28 1/2" square, begin assembly in center of quilt and add borders Q2 to opposite sides of center; then add Q3 borders to top and bottom.

2. Join four sets of eleven fence posts, with Strip Set 1 "rails" between as shown. Join two of these to opposite sides of quilt. Add Unit 4 to opposite short sides of remaining fences, and join to top and bottom of quilt.

3. Join border Q5 to opposite sides of quilt top; then add Q6 border to top and bottom. Join six of Block A in a row, matching seams. Make 4 of these rows. Join two rows to opposite sides of quilt. Join Block B to opposite short ends of remaining Block A rows and add to top and bottom of quilt, matching corner seams.

4. Join Q7 borders to opposite sides of quilt; then join Q8 borders to top and bottom. Join Q9 borders to opposite sides of quilt; then add Q10 borders to top and bottom.

5. Make four rows of 21 fence posts with "rails" between them. Join two of these rows to opposite sides of quilt top. Join Unit Q11 to opposite short sides of remaining two fence rows and join these rows to top and bottom of quilt. Add border Q12 to opposite sides of quilt; then join border Q13 to top and bottom to complete quilt top.

QUILTING AND FINISHING.

The quilt diagram below shows what we did with the quilting on the center of this piece. We used horizontal/vertical grids for the circular center section and a 45° grid on the outside of the circular areas. All of the patchwork was "ditched."

Make approximately 310" of straight-grain, French-fold binding to bind the quilt edges.

of Unit 3 matching. Place the combined leaf units right sides together on violet, raw edges matching. Join the two sections together, matching seams and catching the press on bias into the seam. Open out, and press seam toward flower. Press the bias down. Trim off any excess bias, and top stitch in place.

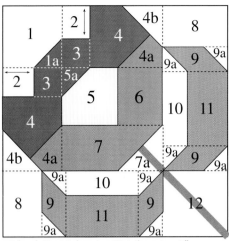

2 1/2" strip
1 1/2" strip
1 1/2" strip

Strip Set 1. Make 5.
Cut into 120 - 1 1/2"
segments for fence.

Piecing Block B

1. Use diagonal corner technique to make four of mirror image Unit 9, two of mirror image Unit 4, and one each of units 5 and 7. Please note, that to make Unit 4, diagonal corners are added in alphabetical order. Also note that this is a mirror image unit.

2. To assemble the block, begin by joining units 2 and 3. Make 2. Join Unit 1 to left side of one 2-3 combined unit. Join Unit 4 to right side. For remaining 2-3 unit, refer to illustration of block above and join remaining Unit 4 to bottom.

3. Join units 5 and 6; then add Unit 7 to bottom of these combined units. Join the 2-4 combined units to left side of combined 5-7 units; then add remaining 1-4 combined units to top, matching seams, to complete the violet.

4. Join both units 10 and 11; then add Unit 9 to opposite short ends of these combined units, keeping in mind that Unit 9 is a mirror image unit. Join Unit 8 to left side of one of the combined 9-11 units; then add to bottom of violet. Join Unit 8 to top of remaining 9-11 units; then add Unit 12 to bottom. Add to right side of violet to complete the block.

5. For the stem, we turned under 1/8" on one short end of press on bias and placed that end at the point where it meets the violet bottom. Press the stem in place, and top stitch with coordinating thread. Make 4 of Block B.

Piecing Block C and Strip Set 1.

1. Use diagonal corner technique to make Unit 1. This is the fence post, and you will make 128 of them. For the rail between the fence posts, refer to illustration of Strip Set 1 above. Join the strips as shown, using anti-directional stitching (explained on page 7) to complete the strip set. Make 5 strip sets. Cut into 120 - 1 1/2" segments as shown for fence rail.

45

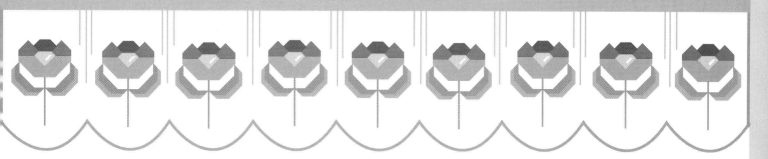

Tablecloth finishes to: 50" square
Block A finishes to 7" x 8 1/4"
Block B finishes to 8 1/4" square.

Techniques used:
Diagonal Corners & Diagonal Ends

MATERIALS FOR TABLECLOTH

☐	Fabric I (white on ivory print)	Need 66 7/8"	2 yards
▦	Fabric II (medium green print)	Need 8 1/2"	3/8 yard
▦	Fabric III (light violet print)	Need 6 1/2"	1/4 yard
▦	Fabric IV (dark violet print)	Need 18 3/4"	5/8 yard
☐	Fabric V (light yellow print)	Need 2 1/4"	1/8 yard
	Backing		3 yards

Violets in the Kitchen

For Embroideries:
Robison Anton #40 weight rayon embroidery thread:
#2424 Cachet (med. violet), #2276 Lavender (lt. Violet),
#2410 Lt. Kelly (med. green), #2211 Nile (lt. Green),
and #2606 TH Gold

> All "Q" units in cutting instructions stand for "quilt top." These are units that are not incorporated into the specific blocks, but are on the quilt top.

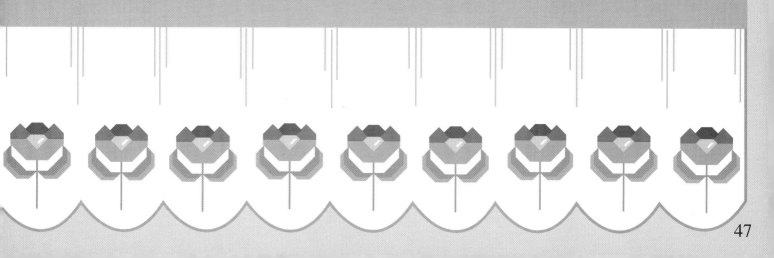

CUTTING FOR TABLECLOTH

From Fabric I, cut: (white on ivory print)
- One 31 1/2"x 42" strip. From this, cut:
    * One – 31 1/2" square (Q1 for embroidery). When embroidery is complete, center and cut down to 28 1/2" square.
    * Thirty-two – 2" sq. (A5a, A9b)
    * Twenty-four – 1 3/4" sq. (B4b, A9a)
    * Thirty-two – 1 1/2" sq. (A2b, A8a)
    * Twenty – 1 1/4" sq. (B9a)
- Two 8 3/4" wide strips. From these, cut:
    * Four – 8 3/4" x 14 1/2" (Q2)
    * Four – 1 3/4" x 8 3/4" (B14)
    * Four – 1 3/4" x 7 1/2" (B13)
    * Eight – 1 3/4" x 3" (A7)
    * Twelve - 1 1/4" sq. (add to B9a)
    * Thirty-two – 1" sq. (A1a, A4b)
- One 2 1/2" wide strip. From this, cut:
    * Four – 2 1/2" sq. (B12)
    * Four – 2 3/8" sq. (B1)
    * Eight – 1 3/4" x 2 1/2" (B8)
    * Four – 1 7/8" sq. (B7a)

- Eight 1 3/4" wide strips. From these, cut:
    * Four – 1 3/4" x 24" (Q4) Piece two together to make two 47 1/2" lengths.
    * Four – 1 3/4" x 22 3/4" (Q3) Piece two together to make two 45" lengths.
    * Eight – 1 1/2" x 7 1/2" (A10)
    * Sixteen – 1 1/2" x 4" (A6)
- One 1 3/8" wide strip. From this, cut:
    * Eight – 1 3/8" x 1 1/2" (B2)
    * Eight – 1 1/4" x 2 3/4" (B10)

From Fabric II, cut: (medium green print)
- Two 2 3/4" wide strips. From these, cut:
    * Sixteen – 2 3/4" sq. (A9)
    * Eight – 1 3/4" x 2 3/4" (B11)
    * Sixteen – 1 1/4" x 2 1/2" (B9)
- Two 1 1/2" wide strips. From this, cut:
    * Thirty-two – 1 1/2" x 1 3/4" (A6a, A8)

From Fabric III, cut: (light violet print)
- Two 2 1/2" wide strips. From these, cut:
    * Sixteen – 2" x 2 1/2" (A5)
    * Four – 1 7/8" x 3 5/8" (B7)
    * Eight – 1 1/2" x 2 1/2" (A3)

48

* Four – 1 7/8" x 2 1/4" (B6)
* Eight – 1 7/8" sq. (B4a)
- One 1 1/2" wide strip. From this, cut:
  * Sixteen – 1 1/2" sq. (A2b)

From Fabric IV, cut: (dark violet print)
- One 2 3/4" wide strip. From this, cut:
  * Eight – 2 3/8" x 2 3/4" (B4)
  * Eight – 1 3/4" x 2 1/2" (A1)
  * Sixteen – 1" sq. (A2a)
- Eight 2" wide strips. From these, cut:
  * Four – 2" x 25 1/2" (Q6) Piece two together to make two 50 1/2" lengths.
  * Four – 2" x 24" (Q5) Piece two together to make two 47 1/2" lengths.
  * Sixteen – 2" x 2 1/4" (A4)
  * Eight – 1 3/4" x 7 1/2" (A11)
  * Sixteen – 1 3/8" sq. (B1a, B3, B5a)

From Fabric V, cut: (light yellow print)
- One 2 1/4" wide strip. From this, cut:
  * Four – 2 1/4" sq. (B5)
  * Eight – 2" x 2 1/2" (A2)

ASSEMBLY

1. The tablecloth blocks are assembled exactly the same as for the quilt. Block A, shown at right has an additional unit (A11) which is added last. Make 8 of Block A.

2. Block B, shown below has two additional units (B13 and B14). Complete the block as for the quilt; then add Unit 13 to top and Unit 14 to left side as shown. Refer to the quilt instructions on pages 44 and 45 for block assembly.

3. The center section is also the same as for the quilt. Refer to instructions on page 44 for the embroidered center.

4. To assemble the tablecloth, make four rows of (Block A, Unit Q2, and Block A). Join two of these rows to opposite sides of the tablecloth. Join Block B to opposite short ends of two remaining Block A-Q2-Block A row; then add to top and bottom of tablecloth. Join Unit Q3 to top and bottom of tablecloth; then add Unit Q4 to opposite sides. Join Unit Q5 to top and bottom of tablecloth; then join Unit Q6 to sides to complete tablecloth.

Block A. Make 8. Finishes to 7" X 8 1/4".

QUILTING AND FINISHING

Quilting is the same as for the quilt (shown on page 45). Cross hatch horizontal/vertical quilting is added to Unit Q2. We used approximately 210" of straight-grain, French fold binding to bind the edges.

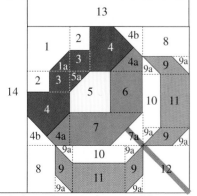

Block B. Make 4. Finishes to 8 1/4" square.

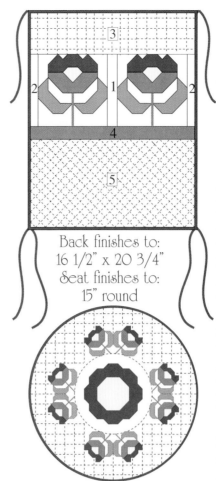

Back finishes to:
16 1/2" x 20 3/4"
Seat finishes to:
15" round

gather ours.

5. Add other embroidered accessories as shown. We made a toaster cover, a bun cover and a dish towel. Dish towel embroidery is from the throw design.

From Fabric III, cut one 2" x 17" strip for Unit Q4.

2. Join the units as shown at left. Cut a backing piece using the seat cover front as a pattern. Quilt with cross hatch design, and bind with approximately 82" of straight-grain binding. Use lavender grosgrain ribbon for chair ties.

3. The embroidery for the chair seat is the same as for the center of the tablecloth. After embroidery is complete, cut a 15 1/2" circle and quilt as shown. Use bias to bind, and use the grosgrain ribbon for ties. We made the round pillow that goes with the quilt in the same manner, however we added a gusset and cording.

4. For the curtains, measure your window and make the number of A blocks needed to span 1 1/2 times the width of your window to allow for gathering. Make the number of A blocks needed for the valance. We did not

Accessories
Chair Back & Seat

1. For the chair back, you will make two of Block A, without Unit 11. For chair back, from Fabric I, cut: One – 1 1/2" x 7 1/2" for Unit Q1. Cut two 1 1/4" x 7 1/2" for Unit Q2. Cut one 4 1/2" x 17" for Unit Q3, and cut one 9" x 17" for Unit Q5.

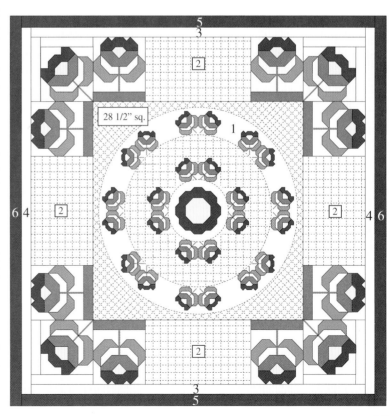

28 1/2" sq.

Cotton Puffs quilt finishes to: 70" x 94"
Block A finishes to 12" x 13 3/4".
Block B finishes to 8" x 12"
Block C finishes to 12" square.

Techniques used: Diagonal Corners, Diagonal Ends, and some "quick piecing" tricks that will surprise you!

For Embroidered Accessories:

Robison Anton #40 weight rayon embroidery thread: #2591 Rose tint (dk. pink), #2580 Green grass (dark green), #2457 Green Dust (medium green), #2211 Nile (light green), and #2732 Pro Maize (yellow).

Cotton Puffs

I consider this to be the "dream" room for any little girl! It's bright! It's a happy place for any young girl whose room is her special, private haven.

Robert's cheerful design, and the color choices for this project give it an individuality for the perfect decor.

In decorating any room, the personality of the person who will spend the most time in that room is the most important factor to be considered. Children respond to a vibrant, colorful environment, where all of their fantasies may be fulfilled.

In setting up this dream room for all to enjoy, our assistant, Gigi Thompson took particular care in finding the accessory items that pulled the continuity of the room together. From the lovely painting of the young girls with the pony, to teddy bears happily riding a tricycle, each element not only fit into the color scheme, but brought the room to life!

MATERIALS

	Fabric I (bright yellow print)	Need 121"	3 1/2 yards
	Fabric II (white on white print)	Need 87"	2 5/8 yards
	Fabric III (pink print)	Need 23 1/2"	3/4 yard
	Fabric IV (dark green print)	Need 67 1/8"	2 yards
	Fabric V (light green print)	Need 47 5/8"	1 1/2 yards
	Backing		6 yards

51

All "Q" units in cutting instructions stand for "quilt top." These are units that are not incorporated into the specific blocks, but are on the quilt top.

Cutting instructions shown in red indicate that the quantity of units is combined and cut in 2 or more different places to conserve fabric.

CUTTING FOR QUILT

☐ **From Fabric I, cut: (bright yellow print)**
- Two 12 1/2" wide strips. From these, cut:
  * Two – 10 1/2" x 12 1/2" (Q1)
  * Eight – 5 1/2" x 12 1/2" (Q2)
  * Twenty-four – 1 3/4" x 3" (C14a, C10)
  * Thirty – 1 1/2" sq. (B2a, B7b, C15b, C17b)
- One 8 1/2" wide strip. From this, cut:
  * Four – 8 1/2" sq. (Q3)
  * Twenty-five – 1 1/2" sq. (add to 1 1/2" sq. above)
- Two 4 1/2" wide strips. From these, cut:
  * Twelve – 4 1/2" sq. (A9)
  * Twelve – 2 1/8" sq. (A6b)
  * Nine – 1 1/2" sq. (add to 1 1/2" sq. above)
- Four 4" wide strips. From these, cut:
  * Forty – 4" sq. (B8)
- One 3 1/2" wide strip. From this, cut:
  * Twelve – 1 3/8" x 3 1/2" (A8a)
  * Eight – 3" sq. (C12)
- One 3 1/4" wide strip. From this, cut:
  * Twelve – 3 1/4" sq. (C18)
- Two 3 1/8" wide strips. From these, cut:
  * Forty – 1 1/4" x 3 1/8" (B6b)
  * Four – 3" sq. (Add to C12 above)
  * Six – 2 3/8" sq. (B6a)
- Five 2 3/4" wide strips. From these, cut:
  * Forty – 2 3/4" x 5" (B4)
- Two 2 5/8" wide strips. From these, cut:
  * Twelve – 2 5/8" x 4 3/4" (A8b)
  * Fifteen – 1 3/4" sq. (A5a, C8a, C13a, C14b, C16b)
- Two 2 3/8" wide strips. From these, cut:
  * Thirty-four – 2 3/8" sq. (add to B6a)
- Three 2 1/4" wide strips. From these, cut:
  * Twenty – 2 1/4" x 4 1/4" (B3)
  * Nineteen – 1 3/4" sq. (add to 1 3/4" sq. above)
- Three 1 3/4" wide strips. From these, cut:
  * Sixty-two – 1 3/4" sq. (add to 1 3/4" sq. above)
- Four 1 1/2" wide strips. From these, cut:
  * Twenty-four – 1 1/2" x 4" (C15, C17a)
  * Forty – 1 1/2" sq. (add to 1 1/2" sq. above)
- Four 1 3/8 " wide strips. From these, cut:
  * Twelve – 1 3/8" x 4 3/8" (A7)
  * Twelve – 1 1/8" x 2 3/8" (B1a)
  * Forty – 1 3/8" sq. (B2b)
- Two 1 1/8" wide strips. From these, cut:
  * Twenty-eight – 1 1/8" x 2 3/8" (add to B1a)

☐ **From Fabric II, cut: (white on white print)**
- Two 4 3/4" wide strips. From these, cut:
  * Twelve – 4 3/4" sq. (C8)
  * Eight – 3" x 4 3/4" (C13)
- Two 4 3/8" wide strips. From these, cut:
  * Twelve – 4 3/8" x 5" (A5)
  * Four – 3" x 4 3/4" (add to (C13)
- Ten 3 1/2" wide strips. From these, cut:
  * Two – 3 1/2" x 42 1/2" (Q5)
  * Four – 3 1/2" x 26 3/4" (Q5) Piece two to opposite short ends of 42 1/2" strip above to make two 94 1/2" lengths.
  * Four – 3 1/2" x 32 1/2" (Q4) Piece two together to make two 64 1/2" lengths.
  * Twelve – 3" x 3 1/2" (C9)

  * Twelve – 1 3/4" x 3" (C14a)
  * Twelve – 1 5/8" sq. (A2a)
  * Thirty-six – 1 1/2" sq. (A2b, C1a, C2a)
- Eight 2 1/2" wide strips for straight-grain binding
- Three 2 1/4" wide strips. From these, cut:
  * Twelve – 2 1/4" x 4 1/2" (C4)
  * Twelve – 2 1/4" x 3 5/8" (A3)
  * Twelve – 2" sq. (C3)
- Three 1 1/2" wide strips. From these, cut:
  * Twelve – 1 1/2" x 4 5/8" (C6)
  * Twelve – 1 1/2" x 2 7/8" (C5)
  * Eight – 1 3/8" x 4" (A7a)
- One 1 3/8" wide strip. From this, cut:
  * Four – 1 3/8" x 4" (Add to A7a)
- One 1 1/8" wide strip. From this, cut:
  * Twelve – 1 1/8" x 2 5/8" (A1a)

☐ **From Fabric III, cut: (pink print)**
- Two 4 1/4" wide strips. From these, cut:
  * Twenty – 3 1/2" x 4 1/4" (B1)
  * Ten – 1 1/2" x 2 3/8" (B2)
- One 4" wide strip. From this, cut:
  * Six – 4" x 4 3/4" (A1)
  * Ten – 1 1/2" x 2 3/8" (add to B2)
- Two 3" wide strips. From these, cut:
  * Twelve – 3" x 4 1/2" (C1)
  * Twelve – 2" x 3" (C2)
- One 2 5/8" wide strip. From this, cut:
  * Twelve – 1 5/8" x 2 5/8" (A2)
- One 2 3/8" wide strip. From this, cut:
  * Twenty – 1 1/2" x 2 3/8" (add to B2)

☐ **From Fabric IV, cut: (dark green print)**
- One 7 7/8" wide strip. From this, cut:
  * Twelve – 2 1/4" x 7 7/8" (C16)
  * Eighteen – 2 1/4" sq. (B4a)
- One 6 5/8" wide strip. From this, cut:
  * Twelve – 2 5/8" x 6 5/8" (A8)
  * Eight – 2 1/4" sq. (add to B4a)
- Three 5 1/2" wide strips. From these, cut:
  * Forty – 2 3/8" x 5 1/2" (B6)
  * Twelve – 2 1/4" x 5 3/8" (C7)
- One 4 3/4" wide strip. From this, cut:
  * Twelve – 3" x 4 3/4" (C14)
- One 4 1/8" wide strip. From this, cut:
  * Twelve – 1 1/2" x 4 1/8" (C6a)
  * Twelve – 1 3/8" x 4" (A7b)
- One 3" wide strip. From this, cut:
  * Twelve – 3" sq. (C11)
- One 2 5/8" wide strip. From this, cut:
  * Twelve – 2" x 2 5/8" (A1a)
  * Ten – 1 3/4" sq. (A6a, B7a)
- Two 2 1/4" wide strips. From these, cut:
  * Twelve – 2" x 2 1/4" (A4)
  * Fourteen – 2 1/4" sq. (add to B4a)
- Eight 1 3/4" wide strips. From these, cut:
  * Forty-two – 1 3/4" sq. (add to A6a, B7a)
  * Forty – 1 3/4" x 2 3/4" (B5)
  * Forty – 1 3/4" x 2 3/8" (B1a)
- One 1 5/8" wide strip. From this, cut:
  * Twelve – 1 5/8" sq. (A3a)
- One 1 1/2" wide strip. From this, cut:
  * Twelve – 1 1/2" x 3 1/8" (C5a)

☐ **From Fabric V, cut: (light green print)**
- One 7 3/8" wide strip. From this, cut:
  * Twelve – 3 3/8" x 7 3/8" (A6)
- One 7 1/4" wide strip. From this, cut:
  * Twenty-four – 1 1/2" x 7 1/4" (C15a, C17)
  * Twenty – 1 1/4" sq. (B5a)

- Three 6 1/2" wide strips. From these, cut:
  * Forty – 2 3/4" x 6 1/2" (B7)
  * Sixteen – 1 5/8" x 3 1/8" (B6b)
- One 3 1/2" wide strip. From this, cut:
  * Twelve – 1 3/4" x 3 1/2" (A8a)
  * Twelve – 1 3/8" sq. (A7c)
  * Twenty – 1 1/4" sq. (add to B5a)
- Three 2 1/4" wide strips. From these, cut:
  * Twenty-four – 2 1/4" x 4 1/8" (C7a, C16a)
  * Eight - 1 5/8" x 3 1/8" (add to B6b)
- Two 1 5/8" wide strips. From these, cut:
  * Sixteen - 1 5/8" x 3 1/8" (add to B6b)

ASSEMBLY

Making Block A

1. Use diagonal corner technique to make two each of units 2, 3, 5, and 6. Use this technique to make one of Unit 1. See diagrams for using our "quick piecing" technique for this unit.

2. Use diagonal end technique to make two each of mirror image units 7 and 8.

3. Unit 1 is made the same for Block A, and Block B, even though small strip set colors and measurements are different. Join the small strip set which will now be used as a diagonal corner. Place

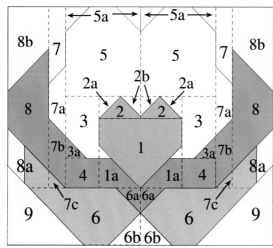

Block A - Make 6 for quilt Finishes to 12" x 13 3/4"

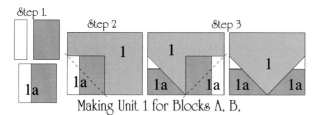

Making Unit 1 for Blocks A, B,

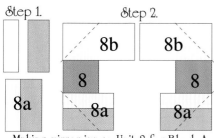

Making mirror image Unit 8 for Block A.

it right sides together on Unit 1 as shown and stitch the diagonal. Trim and press.

4. In making Unit 8, we have done the same thing as with Unit 1, only this time it is a diagonal end. Join the small strip set. Place it right sides together on Unit 8, keeping in mind that the two are mirror images. Stitch the diagonal and press. Place Unit 8 as shown for a right slant and left slant. Stitch, press and trim. Using the strip set as a diagonal corner is a great trick for Flying Geese blocks. Try it and you will be amazed at the variety you will get.

5. Unit 7 is not only a mirror image, but it is a continuous diagonal end as shown on page 8. Refer to illustration for correct placement of mirror image diagonal ends.

6. After all diagonal corner and end units are made, the block may

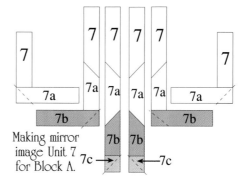

Making mirror image Unit 7 for Block A.

be assembled. Begin by joining the two mirror image units 2. Join these to top of Unit 1 as shown in block diagram. Join mirror image Unit 3 to Unit 4. Join these to opposite sides of combined units 1-2, referring frequently to diagram for correct placement of mirror image units. Join units 5 together, matching seams; then add them to the top of combined units 1-4.

7. Join mirror image units 7 and 8, matching seams. Add these units to opposite sides of the cotton puff as shown. Join units 6 together as shown. Join to bottom of cotton puff. Unit 9 is a diagonal corner which is placed over each bottom corner of the block. Stitch the diagonal, trim seam and press to complete Block A.

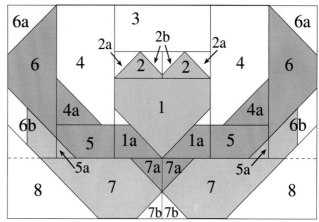

Block B - Make 20 for quilt, 8 for table topper. Finishes to 8" x 12"

Making Block B

1. Use diagonal corner technique to make two each of units 2, 4, 5, and 7. Make one of Unit 1. Please refer to the diagram at left for making Unit 1.

2. Use diagonal end technique to make two of mirror image Unit 6. The assembly is exactly the same as for Block A. Refer to diagram at right for making mirror image Unit 6. Again this assembly is the same as for Unit 8, Block A, however instead of an additional diagonal end, there is a diagonal corner at the top. Complete the strip set diagonal end; then add the diagonal corner.

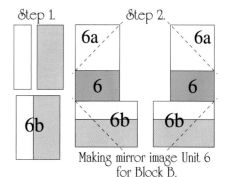

Making mirror image Unit 6 for Block B.

3. To assemble the block, join units 2 together as shown, matching seams. Add these combined units to top of Unit 1; then join Unit 3, making a vertical row. Join mirror image units 4 and 5; then add mirror image Unit 6 to sides of these combined units as shown, matching seams. Join these combined units to opposite sides of center heart section. Join units 7 as illustrated above; then add to bottom of heart section. Unit 8 is a diagonal corner which is placed over each bottom corner of the block. Stitch the diagonal, trim seam and press to complete Block B.

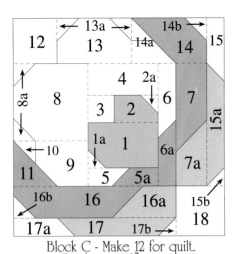
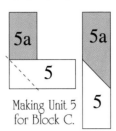

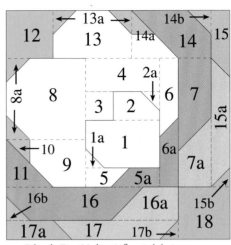

Making Block C

1. Use diagonal corner technique to make one each of units 1, 2, 8, 13, and 14. Use diagonal end technique to make one each of units 5, 6, 7, 15, 16, and 17.

Block C - Make 12 for quilt.
Finishes to 12" square

Making Unit 5 for Block C.

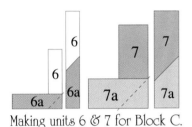

Making units 6 & 7 for Block C.

2. Refer to diagrams for making diagonal end units 5, 6 and 7 so that you obtain the proper slant. To make combined units 9-11, refer to illustration below and begin by joining units 9 and 10 as shown; then add diagonal corner Unit 11.

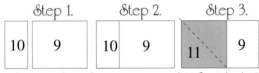

Making combined units 9, 10 and 11 for Block C.

3. Refer to illustration below for making Unit 14. This is a quick piecing technique that can be used in many designs. Join the small strips together for Unit 14a as shown. This is now used as a diagonal corner. Place it right side down on Unit 14 as shown; then stitch the diagonal. Trim seam and press; then add diagonal corner 14b. Trim and press.

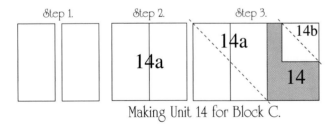

Making Unit 14 for Block C.

4. Refer to illustrations below for making units 15, 16 and 17. Make diagonal ends first; then add diagonal corners.

5. To assemble Block C, begin by joining units 2 and 3; then add Unit 1 to bottom of these combined units. Add Unit 4 to the top as shown. Join Unit 5 to bottom of heart; then add Unit 6 to right side.

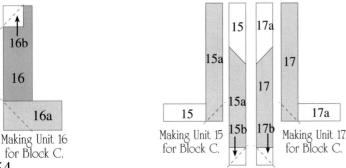

Making Unit 16 for Block C.   Making Unit 15 for Block C.   Making Unit 17 for Block C.

Join Unit 7 to Unit 6 as shown. Join Unit 8 to top of combined units 9-11; then join these combined units to left side of heart section. Join units 12, 13, and 14 in a horizontal row. Add to top of combined heart units; then add Unit 15 to right side.

6. Join units 16 and 17; then join Unit 18 to right side of these combined units. Add these units to bottom of cotton puff to complete the block.

Block D

1. To the left is an illustration of Block D. This block is used for the table topper and for the pillow. It is made exactly the same as for Block C. Refer to the instructions and diagrams for assembling Block C. We have placed the block here for your convenience so that you may refer to the illustrations at left, rather than having to turn pages.

Block D. Make 1 for tabletopper and 1 for pillow. Finishes to 12" square

Quilt Assembly

1. Refer frequently to the quilt diagram on the next page when following these instructions. Begin by joining two groups of four of Block C as shown. Join the two groups together, carefully matching seams.

2. For Block A side rows, join Unit Q2, Block A, Q1, Block A, and Q2 in a row. Make two and join them to opposite sides of center quilt section.

3. Refer to quilt drawing so that you place Block C correctly. Join Block C, Unit Q2, Block A, Unit Q2 and Block C. Make two of these rows and join them to top and bottom of quilt top, matching seams.

4. Make two rows of 6 of Block B, matching leaf seams. Join to opposite sides of quilt top. Make two rows of 4 of Block B; then add Unit Q3 to opposite short ends of the rows. Join these rows to top and bottom of quilt, matching corner seams. Join Unit Q4 border to top and bottom of quilt top; then add previously pieced border Q5 to opposite sides to complete the quilt top.

QUILTING AND FINISHING

There is not enough to say about the superb quilting on this piece. One of the things that we have been doing for photography is adding the quilting in contrasting thread. In this case, Faye used white thread on the yellow, and yellow thread on the white. Although it was for the camera lens, we have decided that it is very appealing as the quilting motifs that are used are as important as the pieced design. They show off beautifully without being gaudy as long as the colors of thread chosen are not too bright.

Faye has feathered hearts all over this quilt top, some of which you can see in the photo. She used a feathered border which set it off beautifully. All of the patchwork was "ditched."

We used approximately 340" of straight-grain, French-fold binding to bind the edges.

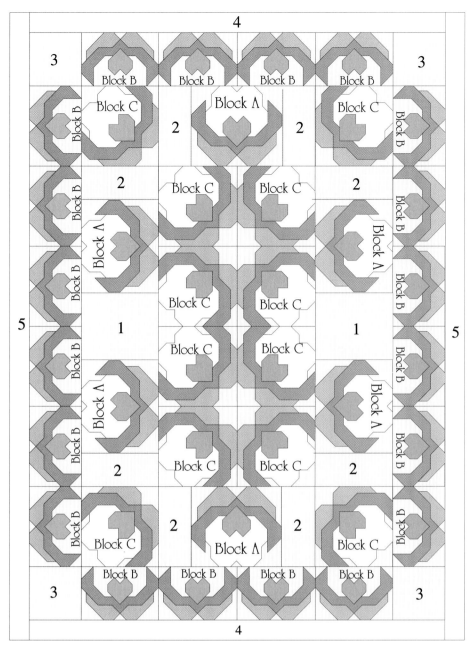

- One 2 3/8" wide strip. From this, cut:
  - Sixteen – 2 3/8" sq. (B6a)
- One 1 3/8" wide strip. From this, cut:
  - Sixteen – 1 3/8" sq. (B2b)

☐ **From Fabric II, cut; (white on white print) You will need 22 3/4" - 3/4 yard.**
- Two 9" wide strips. From these, cut:
  - Eight – 9" sq. for (Q4) embroideries. When embroideries are complete, center and cut down to 4 1/2" squares.
  - Two – 4 1/2" x 8 1/2" (Q3)
- One 4 3/4" wide strip. From this, cut:
  - One – 4 3/4" sq. (D8)
  - One – 3" x 4 3/4" (D13)
  - One – 1 1/2" x 4 5/8" (D6)
  - Two – 4 1/2" x 8 1/2" (Add to Q3)
  - One – 2 1/4" x 4 1/2" (D4)
  - One – 3" x 3 1/2" (D9)
  - One – 1 3/4" x 3" (D14a)
  - One – 1 1/2" x 2 7/8" (D5)
  - One – 2" sq. (D3)
  - Two – 1 1/2" sq. (D1a, D2a)

☐ **From Fabric III, cut: (pink print) You will need 10 1/4" - 3/8 yard.**
- One 4 1/2" wide strip. From this, cut:
  - Four – 4 1/2" sq. (Q5)
  - Six – 3 1/2" x 4 1/4" (B1)
- One 4 1/4" wide strip. From this, cut:
  - Two – 3 1/2" x 4 1/4" (Add to B1)
  - Two – 1 1/2" x 4" (D15, D17a)
  - One – 3 1/4" sq. (D18)
  - One – 3" sq. (D12)
  - Two – 1 3/4" x 3" (D10, D14a)
  - Four – 2 1/2" sq. (Q2)
  - Six – 1 3/4" sq. (D8a, D13a, D14b, D16b)
- One 1 1/2" wide strip. From this, cut:
  - Sixteen – 1 1/2" x 2 3/8" (B2)
  - Two – 1 1/2" sq. (D15b, D17b)

☐ **From Fabric IV, cut: (dark green print) You will need 16" - 1/2 yard.**
- One 5 1/2" wide strip. From this, cut:
  - Sixteen – 2 3/8" x 5 1/2" (B6)
  - One – 3" sq. (D11)
- One 3" wide strip. From this, cut:
  - One – 3" x 4 3/4" (D14)
  - One – 1 1/2" x 4 1/8" (D6a)
  - One – 2 1/4" x 7 7/8" (D16)
  - One – 2 1/4" x 5 3/8" (D7)
  - One – 1 1/2" x 3 1/8" (D5a)
- One 2 1/4" wide strip. From this, cut:
  - Sixteen – 2 1/4" sq. (B4a)
- Three 1 3/4" wide strips. From these, cut:
  - Sixteen – 1 3/4" x 2 3/4" (B5)
  - Sixteen – 1 3/4" x 2 3/8" (B1a)
  - Sixteen – 1 3/4" sq. (B7a)

☐ **From Fabric V, cut: (light green print) You will need 13" - 1/2 yard.**
- Two 6 1/2" wide strips. From these, cut:
  - Sixteen – 2 3/4" x 6 1/2" (B7)
  - Sixteen – 1 5/8" x 3 1/8" (B6b)
  - Two – 2 1/4" x 4 1/8" (D7a, D16a)
  - Two – 1 1/2" x 7 1/4" (D15a, D17)
  - Sixteen – 1 1/4" sq. (B5a)

CUTTING FOR TABLE TOPPER
Table topper finishes to 40" square.

For backing you will need 1 3/8 yards.

☐ **From Fabric I, cut: (bright yellow print) You will need 41 1/8" - 1 1/4 yards.**
- One 8 7/8" wide strip. From this, cut:
  - Two – 8 7/8" sq. (Q6) Cut in half diagonally to = 4 triangles.
  - Eight – 2 1/4" x 4 1/4" (B3)
  - Thirty-two – 1 1/2" sq. (B2a, B7b)
  - One – 3" x 4 1/2" (D1)
  - One – 2" x 3" (D2)
- Two 4" wide strips. From these, cut:
  - Sixteen – 4" sq. (B8)
  - Sixteen – 1 1/8" x 2 3/8" (B1a)
- Two 2 3/4" wide strips. From these, cut:
  - Sixteen – 2 3/4" x 5" (B4)
- Six 2 1/2" wide strips. Four for straight-grain binding. From remaining two, cut:
  - Four – 2 1/2" x 12 1/2" (Q1)
  - Sixteen – 1 1/4" x 3 1/8" (B6b)

55

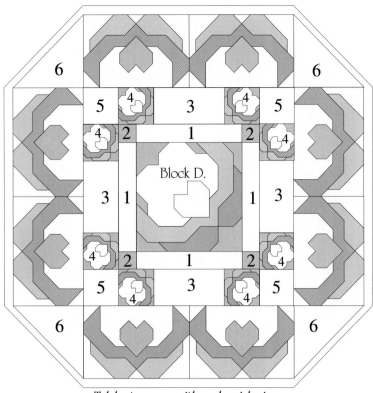

Table topper with embroideries.
Finishes to 40"

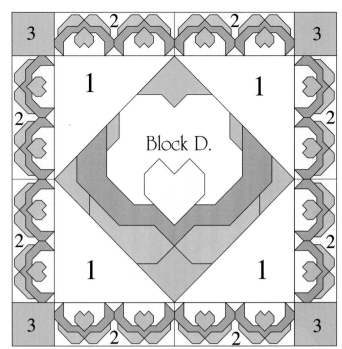

Pillow with embroideries.
Finishes to 23" square.

Making The Table topper

1. Follow instructions and diagrams for quilt blocks B, C, and D, on pages 53 and 54. Make eight of Block B and one of Block D.

2. To assemble the table topper, begin by joining Unit Q1 to top and bottom of Block D. Refer to illustration above for correct position of Block D. Join Units Q2 to opposite short ends of remaining Q1 units; then join them to to opposite sides of Block D, matching corner seams.

3. Join two embroidered Q4 units to opposite sides of all Q3 units. Join two sets to top and bottom of table topper center. Join Unit Q5 to opposite short ends of remaining embroidery rows; then add to opposite sides of center, matching seams.

4. Make four rows of two of Block B. Join to top and bottom of center section. Add triangle Q6 to opposite short ends of remaining two rows; then add to opposite sides to complete table topper.

Quilting and Finishing

The table topper was quilted to match the quilt with feathered motifs. We used Fabric II to bind the edges with bias binding.

CUTTING FOR "Q" UNITS OF PILLOW
Pillow finishes to 23" square

Fabric I (bright yellow print)   Need 109"   3 1/8 yards

Fabric II (white on white print)   Need 9 3/8"   1/2 yard

Fabric III (pink print)   Need 3 1/2"   1/8 yard

Follow instructions for making one block on page 11, and make one of Block D. Instructions and illustrations for Block D are on page 54.

Cutting instructions below are for all "Q" units and for Fabric I to be embroidered.

From Fabric I, cut:
• Two 14 1/2" wide strips. From these, cut:
    * Two – 14 1/2" x 23 1/2" (pillow backing)
    * Two – 12" x 16" (Q2 for embroideries) When embroideries are complete, center, and cut down to 3 1/2" x 9"
• Five 16" wide strips. From these, cut:
    * Six – 12" x 16" (add to Q2)

From Fabric II, cut:
• Two – 9 3/8" squares (Q1) Cut in half diagonally to = 4 triangles.

From Fabric III, cut:
• Four – 3 1/2" sq. (Q3)

ASSEMBLY

1. Turn Block D "on point" and join Unit Q1 triangles around the block as shown, making it a square.

2. Join Q2 embroidery units together, making four rows of two, being sure to match leaves. Join embroidered rows to top and bottom of pillow. Join Unit Q3 to opposite short sides of remaining two embroidered rows; then add to opposite sides of pillow to complete the top.

3. For pillow backing, press under 1/4" twice on one 23 1/2" side of each pillow backing piece. Top stitch in place. Place the two pillow backs face down on pillow front, overlapping hemmed edges, and pin. Use 1/4" seam and stitch around outer edge of pillow. Turn right side out and press.

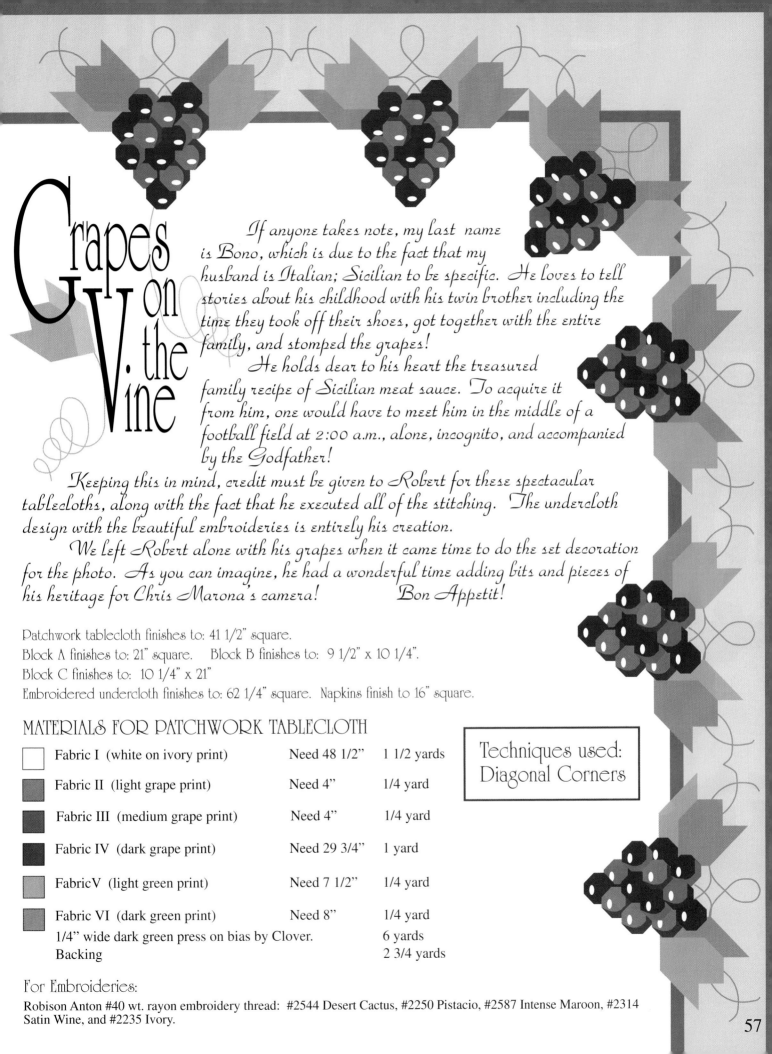

Grapes on the Vine

If anyone takes note, my last name is Bono, which is due to the fact that my husband is Italian; Sicilian to be specific. He loves to tell stories about his childhood with his twin brother including the time they took off their shoes, got together with the entire family, and stomped the grapes!

He holds dear to his heart the treasured family recipe of Sicilian meat sauce. To acquire it from him, one would have to meet him in the middle of a football field at 2:00 a.m., alone, incognito, and accompanied by the Godfather!

Keeping this in mind, credit must be given to Robert for these spectacular tablecloths, along with the fact that he executed all of the stitching. The undercloth design with the beautiful embroideries is entirely his creation.

We left Robert alone with his grapes when it came time to do the set decoration for the photo. As you can imagine, he had a wonderful time adding bits and pieces of his heritage for Chris Marona's camera!   Bon Appetit!

Patchwork tablecloth finishes to: 41 1/2" square.

Block A finishes to: 21" square.   Block B finishes to: 9 1/2" x 10 1/4".

Block C finishes to: 10 1/4" x 21"

Embroidered undercloth finishes to: 62 1/4" square. Napkins finish to 16" square.

MATERIALS FOR PATCHWORK TABLECLOTH

☐ Fabric I (white on ivory print)	Need 48 1/2"	1 1/2 yards
☐ Fabric II (light grape print)	Need 4"	1/4 yard
☐ Fabric III (medium grape print)	Need 4"	1/4 yard
☐ Fabric IV (dark grape print)	Need 29 3/4"	1 yard
☐ Fabric V (light green print)	Need 7 1/2"	1/4 yard
☐ Fabric VI (dark green print)	Need 8"	1/4 yard
1/4" wide dark green press on bias by Clover.		6 yards
Backing		2 3/4 yards

> Techniques used:
> Diagonal Corners

For Embroideries:

Robison Anton #40 wt. rayon embroidery thread: #2544 Desert Cactus, #2250 Pistacio, #2587 Intense Maroon, #2314 Satin Wine, and #2235 Ivory.

Cutting instructions shown in red indicate that the quantity of units is combined and cut in 2 or more different places to conserve fabric.

CUTTING FOR PATCHWORK TABLECLOTH

From Fabric I, cut: (white on ivory print)
- One 9 1/2" wide strip. From this, cut:
  * Eight – 4 3/4" x 9 1/2" (C6)
  * Thirty-six – 1" sq. (A6a, A14a, B6a, C15a, C19a)
- One 5 1/2" wide strip. From this, cut:
  * Four – 1" x 5 1/2" (C23)
  * Eight – 3/4" x 5 1/2" (C21)
  * Four – 2 1/2" x 4" (A18)
  * Twelve – 3/4" x 4" (A17, B13)
  * Four – 3/4" x 3 3/4" (A16)
- From scrap, cut:
  * Fifty – 1" sq. (add to 1" sq. above)
- Five 2 1/2" wide strips. From these, cut:
  * Twenty – 2 1/2" x 6" (A19, B9, B10, C17)
  * Four – 2 1/2" x 4 1/2" (B14)
  * Twenty – 2 1/2" sq. (A8, B8, C9)
  * Fourteen – 1 1/2" x 2 1/2" (A4, A12, B4)
- One 2 1/4" wide strip. From this, cut:
  * Four – 2 1/4" sq. (A15)
  * Sixteen – 2" x 2 1/4" (C22)
- Five 2" wide strips. From these, cut:
  * Seventy-two – 2" sq. (A1a, A5a, A9a, A13a, B1a, B5a, C1a, C11a, C12a, C13a, C14a)
  * Sixty-four – 3/4" x 2" (A7, B7, C16, C20)
  * Thirty-six – 1" sq. (add to 1" sq. above)
- Three 1 1/2" wide strips. From these, cut:
  * Eight – 1 1/2" x 6" (C18)
  * Two – 1 1/2" x 2 1/2" (add to A4, A12, B4)
  * Thirty-two – 1 1/2" sq. (A2, A10, B2, C7)
  * Four – 3/4" x 3 1/2" (C5)
  * Sixteen – 1" sq. (add to 1" sq. above)
- One 1 1/4" wide strip. From this, cut:
  * Sixteen – 1 1/4" sq. (C2a, C3)
  * Twenty-two – 1" sq. (add to 1" sq. above)
- Three 1" wide strips. From these, cut:
  * Four – 1" x 3 1/2" (C4)
  * Eighty – 1" sq. (add to 1" sq. above)

From Fabric II, cut: (light grape print)
- Two 2" wide strips. From these, cut:
  * Thirty – 2" sq. (A6, A14, B6, C15)

From Fabric III, cut: (medium grape print)
- Two 2" wide strips. From these, cut:
  * Two – 2" x 21 1/2" (A21)
  * Two – 2" x 18 1/2" (A20)

From Fabric IV, cut: (dark grape print)
- Two 3 1/4" wide strips. From these, cut:
  * Four – 3 1/4" x 10 3/4" (B16)
  * Four – 3 1/4" x 8" (B15)
- One 2 3/4" wide strip. From this, cut:
  * Twelve – 2 3/4" sq. (B11, C6a)
- Five 2 1/2" wide strips for straight-grain binding.
- Two 2" wide strips. From these, cut:
  * Thirty – 2" sq. (A6, A14, B12, C19)
- Four 1" wide strips. From these, cut:
  * Four – 1" x 21 1/2" (C24)

From Fabric V, cut: (light green print)
- One 4" wide strip. From this, cut:
  * Fourteen – 2" x 4" (A9, C14)
  * Four – 3 1/4" x 3 1/2 " (C1)

- One 2" wide strip. From this, cut:
  * Fourteen – 2" x 2 1/2" (A13, C12)
  * Four – 1 1/4" x 2" (C2)
- One 1 1/2" wide strip. From this, cut:
  * Fourteen – 1 1/2" sq. (A11, C10)
  * Eight – 1 1/4" sq. (C3)

From Fabric VI, cut: (dark green print)
- One 4" wide strip. From this, cut:
  * Eighteen – 2" x 4" (A1, B1, C13)
- One 2 1/2" wide strip. From this, cut:
  * Eighteen – 2" x 2 1/2" (A5, B5, C11)
- One 1 1/2" wide strip. From this, cut:
  * Eighteen – 1 1/2" sq. (A3, B3, C8)

ASSEMBLY
Techniques used: Diagonal Corners and Triangle Squares

We are beginning the assembly instructions with Making Block B for ease in referring to the block diagram below. Block A instructions are on following page.

Making Block B
1. Use diagonal corner technique to make two of Unit 6. Make one each of units 1, 5, and 12.
2. To assemble the block, begin by joining units 2 and 3; then add Unit 4 to left side of combined 2-3 units. Join Unit 5 to bottom; then add Unit 1 to right side as shown. Join Unit 7 to opposite sides of one grape Unit 6; then add Unit 8 to the top. Add these combined units to right side of leaf section.
3. Join Unit 9 to top of leaf section; then add Unit 10 to left side. Using diagonal corner technique, join Unit 11 as shown.
4. Join grape Unit 6, Unit 7, grape Unit 12, and Unit 7 in a horizontal row. Join Unit 13 to top and bottom of the grape row as shown. Join Unit 14 to left side of grape row; then add to bottom of leaf section.
5. Join Unit 15 to top of Block B; then add Unit 16 to left side to complete the block. Make 4.

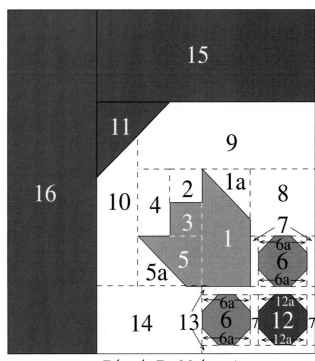

Block B. Make 4.
Finishes to 9 1/2” x 10 1/4”.

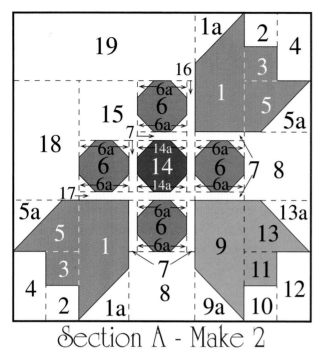

Section A - Make 2

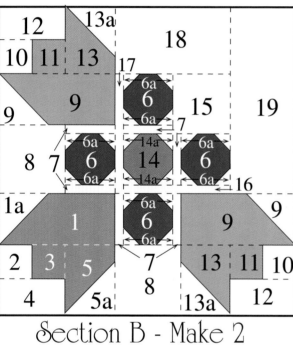

Section B - Make 2

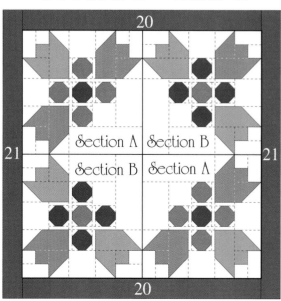

Please note that some units that divide the grapes are small, however if accurate 1/4" seams are taken, they will fit, and the results are stunning.

Making Block A

Block A is divided into two sections that are shown at left. There are two of each section. The entire block drawing is shown at the bottom of the page. Assembly instructions for diagonal corners are given for both A and B Sections.

1. Use diagonal corner technique to make a total of twenty grape units (6 and 14, ten of each color). Make six each of units 1, 5, 9, and 13.

2. To assemble Section A, begin with dark green leaves and join units 2 and 3. Join Unit 4 to side of combined 2-3 units as shown; then add Unit 5 to combined 2-4 units. Join Unit 1 to long side of these combined units to complete the dark green leaf. Make all six dark green leaves for Section A and Section B.

3. For the light green leaf, begin by joining units 10 and 11; then add Unit 12 as shown. Join Unit 13 to combined units; then add Unit 9 to long side of combined 10-13 units to complete the light green leaf. Make all six light green leaves for both sections.

4. Referring to diagram of Section A at left, join Unit 7 to opposite sides of two Unit 6 grapes. Join Unit 8 to these combined units as shown. Make 2. Join one of these sets between one dark green leaf and one light green leaf (horizontally) as shown. Join remaining 6-8 unit to remaining dark green leaf and set aside. Join a row of one light grape Unit 6, Unit 7, and the dark grape Unit 14. Join remaining Unit 7 to bottom of remaining light grape Unit 6. Add Unit 15 to left side of 6-7 combined units. Join the 6-7-15 combined units to the light and dark grape row as shown. Join Unit 16 along right side of the grape row; then add Unit 17 to to the bottom. Join Unit 18 to the left side of the center combined units; then add Unit 19 to the top as illustrated.

6. Join the dark leaf that is combined with the 6-7-8 units to the right side of the center section; then join the remaining leaf/grape/leaf row to the bottom to complete Section A. Make two of this section.

7. Section B is made exactly the same as Section A, only the leaf and grape colors are reversed. Follow Step 4, and join the remaining 6-8 units to remaining <u>light</u> green leaf. For center section, refer to Section B illustration. Join a row of one light grape Unit 14, Unit 7, and the dark grape Unit 6. Join Unit 7 to bottom of remaining dark grape Unit 6. Add Unit 15 to right side of 6-7 combined units. Join the 6-7-15 combined units to the light and dark grape row as shown. Join Unit 16 along bottom of the grape row; then add Unit 17 to to left side. Join Unit 18 to the top of the center combined units; then add Unit 19 to the right as illustrated.

8. Join the light leaf that is combined with the 6-7-8 units to the left side of the center section; then join the remaining leaf/grape/leaf row to the bottom to complete Section B. Make two of this section.

9. Referring to block diagram, join the sections together as shown. Join Unit 20 border to top and bottom; then add Unit 21 to opposite sides to complete Block A.

Making Block C

1. Use diagonal corner technique to make four of unit 19, three of Unit 15, two each of units 6, 11, 12, 13, and 14. Use this technique to make one each of units 1 and 2.

2. Unit 3 is a triangle-square. Refer to illustration below for assembly, and make eight.

Use this assembly for Block C, Unit 3.

Place 1 1/4" squares of fabrics I and V right sides together, matching raw edges, and stitch a diagonal line down the center as shown. Press open and trim center seam, leaving the top and base fabric.

3. To assemble the block, refer to diagram on the following page, and begin by joining Unit 3 to opposite sides of Unit 2, keeping in mind that Unit 3 is sewn as a mirror image. Join Unit 4 to top of combined units, and Unit 1 to bottom. Join Unit 5 to bottom of Unit 1; then join mirror image Unit 6 to opposite sides of combined 1-5 units. Join Unit 24 across the top as shown.

4. To make the leaves, refer frequently to illustration for correct placement of mirror image units. Begin by joining units 7 and 8. Join another Unit 7 to Unit

10 as shown. Join these combined units to opposite sides of Unit 9. Remember correct placement, these are mirror image units. Join units 11 and 12; join them to the bottom of combined units 7-10. Join Unit 13 to one side of these combined units, and Unit 14 to the other side. Join Unit 16 to top and bottom of two light grapes, (Unit 15); then add Unit 17 to these combined units, referring to diagram for correct placement of mirror image units. Add these combined units to bottom of combined leaf units; then join Unit 18 to each leaf section as shown.

5. For grape cluster, make a vertical center row by joining dark grape Unit 19, Unit 20, light grape Unit 15, Unit 20, and dark grape Unit 19. Join Unit 21 to opposite long sides of this row. Make two vertical rows of Unit 22, dark grape Unit 19, and Unit 22. Join

these to opposite sides of center grape row as shown; then add Unit 23 to bottom to complete grape cluster.

6. To assemble the complete block, join mirror image leaf sections to opposite sides of center grape cluster; then add to bottom of combined top units. Make 4 of Block C.

Patchwork Tablecloth Assembly

1. Refer to drawing at left for complete tablecloth assembly. Join Block C to top and bottom of Block A. Join Block B to opposite short sides of two remaining Block C's, matching the diagonal seams. Join to opposite sides of center section, again matching seams.

2. For the vines, use 1/4" wide press on bias made by Clover. We drew the lines with a blue water soluble pen; then pressed the bias down over our lines. If you choose to make your own press on bias, refer to our instructions on page 30. We top stitched the bias in place along edges and used a wide zig zag stitch on the short ends to keep it from fraying.

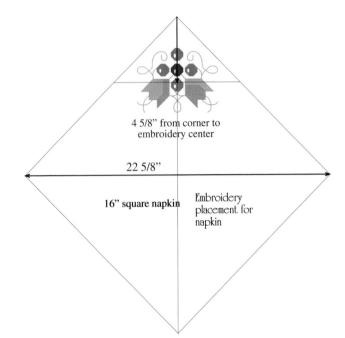

4 5/8" from corner to embroidery center

22 5/8"

16" square napkin

Embroidery placement for napkin

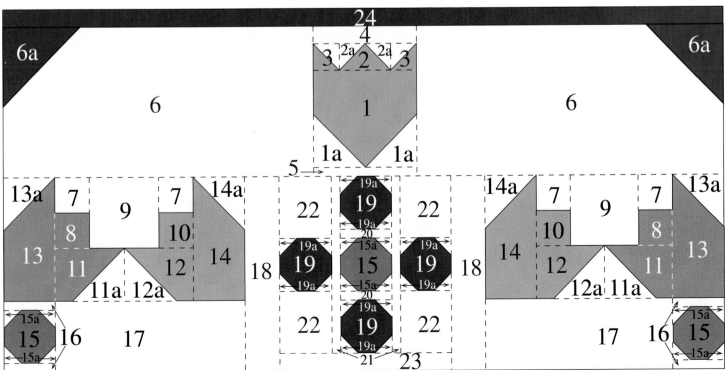

Block C. Make 4. Finishes to 10 1/4" x 21".

Undercloth. Finishes to 62 1/4" sq.

* We used a flannel sheet rather than batting for quilting this tablecloth. If you use a flannel sheet, be sure to wash it first as it shrinks differently than your cotton fabrics.

CUTTING FOR EMBROIDERED TABLECLOTH

From Fabric I, cut: (white on ivory print) You will need 215" - 6 1/8 yards.
• Eleven 16" wide strips. From these, cut:
* Thirty-two – 12" x 16" (for embroideries). When embroideries are complete, center and cut down to 5 1/8" x 6 1/2". *Please note that we alternated colors on the grapes.
* Four – 5 1/8" squares for triangle-square corners
• Six 6 1/2" wide strips. From these, cut:
* Two – 6 1/2" x 36 1/2" (side inner borders)
* Four – 6 1/2" x 24 1/2" (top and bottom inner borders). Piece two together to = two 48 1/2" lengths.

From Fabric II, cut: (light grape print) You will need 1 1/8 yards.
• One 36 1/2" square for tablecloth center.

From Fabric III, cut: (medium grape print) You will need 29 1/8" - 7/8 yard.
• One 5 1/8" wide strip. From this, cut:
* Four – 5 1/8" squares for triangle-square corners.
• Eight 3" wide strips. From these, cut:
* Four – 3" x 31 5/8" (side outer borders) Piece two together to = two 62 3/4" lengths.
* Four – 3" x 29 1/8" (top and bottom outer borders) Piece two together to = two 57 14" lengths.

From Fabric IV, cut: (dark grape print) You will need 15" - 1/2 yard.
• Six 2 1/2" wide strips for straight-grain binding.

You will need 3 3/4 yards for backing.

ASSEMBLY

1. After embroidery is complete and embroidered blocks trimmed, join eight grape blocks, alternating the grape colors.
2. Join the side inner borders to opposite sides of the 32 1/2" center square. Join the top and bottom inner borders. Join one row of grape blocks to opposite sides of tablecloth.
3. Refer to page 8 for our method of making half square triangles. Make the corner half square triangles and join them to opposite short ends of the two remaining embroidered grape rows. Join to top and bottom of tablecloth.
4. Join the top and bottom outer borders; then add the side outer borders to complete the tablecloth.

QUILTING & FINISHING FOR BOTH TABLECLOTHS

For the patchwork tablecloth, all of the patchwork and the bias vines were "ditched." In empty spaces on both tablecloths, Faye quilted grape leaves and clusters of grapes.

We used approximately 175" of straight-grain French-fold binding for the patchwork tablecloth, and 260" for the embroidered tablecloth.

NAPKINS

Refer to page 61 for embroidery placement on napkins.
For embroidery on Fabric II napkins, use Robison Anton #2316 Celery for outer grapes and Pistachio #2250 for center grape.

For reversible napkins, cut two 16" squares for the napkins, from Fabrics I and II. Place them wrong sides together and bind with French-fold binding from Fabric IV.

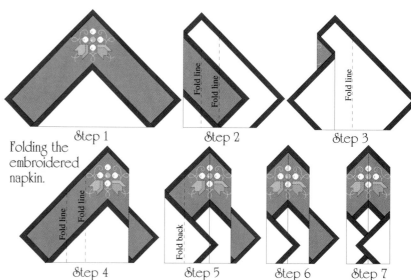

Folding the embroidered napkin.

Step 1 Step 2 Step 3
Step 4 Step 5 Step 6 Step 7

Fleur-de-Lis

Quilts are tailor made to decorate any room in the house. In this case, we have used our Fleur-de-Lis design to enhance this guest bath.

I always notice unique decorating styles used by many Bed & Breakfasts throughout the world; particularly those in which they carry the theme from bedroom to bath. May it be warm and cozy, or elegant and sophisticated, each room the guest enters exudes the same comfortable or luxurious mood.

Coordinated accessories and colors are the most important parts of pulling an overall theme together. Candles, especially in the bath add to the feeling, giving a warm, rich glow. Rolling your towels, and tying them with ribbons is a great way to make your guests feel that you have taken special care, keeping their comfort in mind.

Our young secretary, Sarah, added her personal touch to the decor of our bath by bringing a green garter she had worn to her Senior Prom, and placed it around a rolled, ivory towel. Sarah proved that items you would ordinarily discard after a special occasion, can be the final creative touches that give your room its own personality.

Shower curtain finishes to: 60" x 72 1/2"
Valance finishes to 10" x 60"
Block A finishes to: 8 1/4" square.

> Techniques used:
> Diagonal Corners and
> Strip Sets

MATERIALS

☐	Fabric I (ivory with green print)	Need 156 1/8"	4 5/8 yards
☐	Fabric II (gold print)	Need 34 3/4"	1 1/8 yards
☐	Fabric III (medium olive print)	Need 20"	5/8 yards
☐	Fabric IV (dark rust print)	Need 109"	4 1/4 yards
	Backing		4 1/4 yards

For Embroideries:

Robison Anton #40 weight rayon embroidery thread: #2606 TH Gold, #2493 Light bronze, #2522 Bridgeport Blue, #2275 Slate Blue, #2250 Pistacio, #2454 Fleece Green.

All "Q" units in cutting instructions stand for "quilt top." These are units that are not incorporated into the specific blocks, but are on the quilt top.

Cutting instructions shown in red indicate that the quantity of units is combined and cut in 2 or more different places to conserve fabric.

CUTTING

☐ **From Fabric I, cut: (ivory with green print)**
- Six 8 3/4" wide strips. From these, cut:
  * Twenty-four – 8 3/4" sq. (Q1)
  * 336 – 1" sq. (A4a)
- Two 6" wide strips. From these, cut:
  * Two – 6" x 29 3/8" (Q2) Piece together to = one 58 1/4" length.
  * 144 – 1" sq. (add to A4a above)
- Seven 2 1/2" wide strips for straight-grain binding.
- Six 2" wide strips for Strip Sets 2 and 3.
- Twenty-three 1 3/4" wide strips. From these, cut:
  * 256 – 1 3/4" x 1 7/8" (A2)
  * 256 – 1 3/4" sq. (A1a)
- Four 1 5/8" wide strips. From these, cut:
  * Four – 1 5/8" x 36 3/4" (Q4) Piece together to = two 73" lengths.
  * Twenty – 1" sq. (Add to A4a above)
- Two 1 1/2" wide strips. From these, cut:
  * Two – 1 1/2" x 29 3/8" (Q3) Piece together to = one 58 1/4" length.
  * Twelve – 1" sq. (Add to A4a)
- Nine 1 3/8" wide strips. From these, cut:
  * 256 – 1 3/8" sq. (A7a)

▨ **From Fabric II, cut: (gold print)**
- Eight 2 1/4" wide strips. From these, cut:
  * 128 – 2 1/4" sq. (A1)
- Ten 1 3/8" wide strips for Strip Sets 1 and 2.
- Three 1" strips for Strip Set 3.

▨ **From Fabric III, cut: (medium olive print)**
- Eight 2 1/2" wide strips. From these, cut:
  * 128 – 2 1/2" sq. (A7)

■ **From Fabric IV, cut: (dark rust print)**
- Cut a 62 1/2" length. From this, cut:
  * One – 14" x 62 1/2" (for embroidered valance)
- After embroidered valance is trimmed, press it, and place it right sides together on remaining 62 1/2" length, using it as a template for cutting the lining. Cut the lining.
- From remaining 62 1/2" length, cut:
  * Five – 2 1/2" x 62 1/2" strips for straight-grain binding.
  * 248 – 1" squares (A2a)
- Two 7 1/2" x 42" strips. From these, cut:
  * Fourteen – 4 1/2" x 7 1/2" for loops.
  * 133 – 1" sq. (add to A2a)
- Ten 2 1/4" wide strips. From these, cut:
  * 256 – 1 1/2" x 2 1/4" (A4)
  * Seventy-two – 1" sq. (add to A2a)
* Nine 1" wide strips. Seven for Strip Set 1. From remaining two strips, cut:
  * Fifty-nine – 1" sq. (add to A2a)

ASSEMBLY

Making The Strip Sets
1. Refer to diagram at top of page and make the strip sets as directed. Cut the correct amount and size of segments, and put each strip set into a zip top plastic bag and label it.
2. Refer to Block A illustration on page 66. Use diagonal corner technique to make eight each of units 2 and 4. Make four each of

Strip Set 1		Strip Set 2		Strip Set 3	
1"	1 3/8"	1 3/8"	2"	1"	2"

Make 7.
Cut into 256
7/8" segments

Make 3.
Cut into 128
7/8" segments

Make 3.
Cut into 128
7/8" segments

units 1 and 7.
3. To assemble the block, begin by joining all four of Unit 1 as shown to complete the center of the block. Join Units 2 together as shown. Join Unit 3 to opposite sides of all joined Units 2, matching seams. Join Unit 4 together as shown; then add to top of Unit 1-3 combined units, forming a heart shape.
4. Join two of the combined 2-3-4 sections to opposite sides of center portion of block, matching seams.
5. Referring to leaf drawing at top left corner of Block A, join Unit 6 to right side of each Unit 7 leaf. Join Unit 5 to bottom as shown. Make four of these corners. Join the corner sections to opposite short sides of remaining 2-3-4 joined units; then add to top and bottom of block, matching seams to complete Block A. Make 32.

Making The Top
1. Refer to illustration of complete shower curtain on page 67. Beginning at top of shower curtain, make a row of four Block A with Q1 blocks between. Make four rows. Make a row of Q1 blocks with A blocks between. Make three rows. Make one row of seven of Block A for bottom of shower curtain. Join the rows together as shown in the drawing, matching corner seams.
2. Unit Q2 can not be seen on the illustration as it is under the valance. Join it to the top of the shower curtain. Join Unit Q3 to the bottom; then add Unit Q4 to each side to complete the shower curtain top.

Making The Valance
1. Refer to illustration of valance on page 66 for placement of embroideries. If you are making a plain valance of coordinating fabrics, it may be cut the same way and sewn into the shower curtain in the same manner.
2. Stitch the embroideries and cut the valance as instructed in the illustration. Place it right sides together on lining fabric and cut the lining. Stitch around the bottom of the valance. Clip seams, turn right side out and press. Set aside until shower curtain is quilted.

QUILTING & FINISHING

* We used a flannel sheet rather than batting for quilting the shower curtain. If you use a flannel sheet, be sure to wash it first as it will shrink differently than your cotton fabrics. It will drape better if the flannel is used.

When Faye and I laid the shower curtain top out in her studio, we both noticed the Fleur-de-Lis stencil at the same time. This was used in all of the blank blocks and the patchwork was "ditched."

1. After quilting, trim the shower curtain backing and flannel or batting even with top. Be sure that the valance is pressed.
2. Baste the valance securely along the top and side raw edges of the shower curtain. We used approximately 275" of straight-grain, French-fold binding. The valance was bound into the shower curtain along the top and side edges.
3. For the loops, press under 1/4" on one short edge. Fold loop in half lengthwise, right sides together and stitch around one short raw edge, and long side. Turn right side out and press. Complete fourteen of the loops.
4. Space loops apart evenly on shower curtain top, beginning and ending at ends of shower curtain as shown on page 67. Loops should be placed with short raw edge 1/4" above binding on top front side of shower curtain, with loop hanging down towards valance bottom.

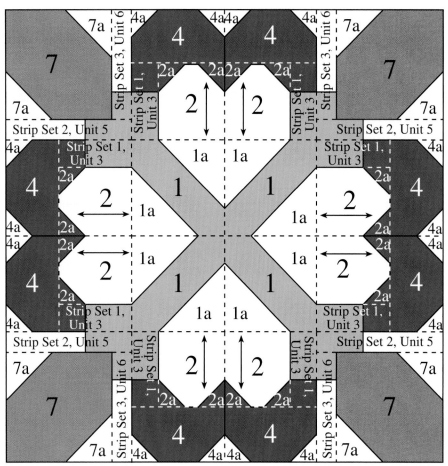

Block A. Make 32. Finishes to 8 1/4" sq.

5. Stitch the raw edge of the loop through all thicknesses. Press it upwards. Bring the loop over to the back side and slip stitch in place on back side just below binding.

* Please note that ⟷ shown on any unit indicates the longest side of the unit. We show this when difference of measurement (length and width) is only 1/8".

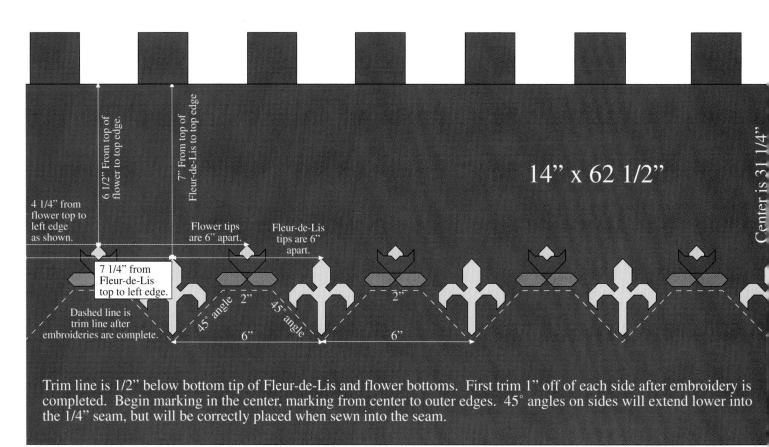

Trim line is 1/2" below bottom tip of Fleur-de-Lis and flower bottoms. First trim 1" off of each side after embroidery is completed. Begin marking in the center, marking from center to outer edges. 45° angles on sides will extend lower into the 1/4" seam, but will be correctly placed when sewn into the seam.

Embroidery placement. Valance for shower curtain finishes to 10" x 60"

Shower curtain finishes to 60" x 72 1/2"

Baltimore Roses

Baltimore Roses exceeded all of our expectations in every way. The blending of beautiful embroideries with elegant patchwork and the quilting of a true artist, made this project special for everyone who worked on it.

If you do not own an embroidery machine, the quilting designs provided with this project, will most certainly give the desired effect.

For Embroideries:

Robison Anton #40 weight rayon embroidery thread:
#2311 Seafoam Green, #2597 Jungle Green (dark green),
#2223 Pink (lt. pink), #2591 Rose Tint (dark pink),
#2252 Russet (burgundy), #2335 Ivory, and #2606 TH Gold.

Techniques used:
Diagonal Corners, Diagonal Ends, Half
Square Triangles, and Strip Sets

MATERIALS FOR QUILT

■	Fabric I (dark burgundy print)	Need 156 1/4"	4 1/2 yards
■	Fabric II (medium rose print)	Need 90 1/8"	2 5/8 yards
▢	Fabric III (light rose print)	Need 36 3/4"	1 1/8 yards
▢	Fabric IV (medium green print)	Need 58"	1 3/4 yards
▢	Fabric V (white on white print)	Need 86 1/2"	2 5/8 yards
▢	Fabric VI (medium gold print)	Need 7 1/2"	1/4 yard
	Backing		7 1/2 yards

CUTTING FOR QUILT

 From Fabric I, cut: (dark burgundy print)
• Two 5" wide strips. From these, cut:
   * Twelve – 5" sq. (Q1)
   * Twenty – 1 1/8" x 3 1/4" (A12)
• One 3 1/4" wide strip. From this, cut:
   * Twenty-eight – 1 1/8" x 3 1/4" (add to A12)
• Twenty 2 1/2" wide strips. Ten strips for straight-grain binding. From remaining ten strips, cut:
   * Two – 2 1/2" x 42" (outer side borders)
   * Four – 2 1/2" x 41 1/2" (outer top & bottom borders) Piece two together to = 82 1/2"
   * Four – 2 1/2" x 31 1/2" (outer side borders) Join to opposite short ends of 42" long strip to = 104" long border. Make 2.
• Eight 2 3/8" wide strips for Strip Set 1.
• Six 2 1/4" wide strips. From these, cut:
   * Ninety-six – 2 1/4" sq. (A2b, A13b)
   * Forty-four – 1 1/8" sq. (B1a, B4b)
• Six 2" wide strips. From these, cut:
   * Ninety-six – 2" sq. (A2a, A13a)
   * Forty-eight – 1 1/8" x 2" (A9)
• Eight 1 3/4" wide strips. From these, cut:
   * 192 – 1 3/4" sq. (B2, B5)
• Seven 1 5/8" wide strips. From these, cut:
   * Ninety-six – 1 5/8" sq. (A1a, A14a)
   * Ninety-six - 1 1/4" x 1 5/8" (A7)
• Eight 1 1/4" strips. From these, cut:
   * 240 – 1 1/4" sq. (A3, A4a, A5a, A6)
   * Fourteen – 1 1/8" sq. (add to B1a, B4b)
• Nine 1 1/8" wide strips. From these, cut:
   * Forty-eight – 1 1/8" x 1 3/4" (A11)
   * 230 – 1 1/8" sq. (add to B1a, B4b)
• Three 1" wide strips. From these, cut:
   * Ninety-six – 1" sq. (A8a, A10a)

From Fabric II, cut: (medium rose print)
• Three 19" wide strips. From these, cut:
   * Five – 19" sq. for embroideries. See illustration. After embroideries are complete, cut in half diagonally to = 10 triangles for large triangle borders.
   * One – 17 1/2" square for corner embroideries. Refer to illustration for embroidery placement. When embroidery is complete, cut off 2" all the way around square; then cut

square in half diagonally.
   * Eleven – 3 1/8" x 5" (A1).
• One 17 1/2" wide strip. From this cut:
   * One – 17 1/2" square. (Add to other 17 1/2" sq. for corner embroideries).
   * Twenty – 3 1/8" x 5" (add to A1)
• Five 3 1/8" wide strips. From these, cut:
   * Forty-eight – 2 3/8" x 3 1/8" (A14)
   * Seventeen – 3 1/8" x 5" (add to A1)

From Fabric III, cut: (light rose print)
• Seven 2 3/4" wide strips. From these, cut:
   * Ninety-six – 2 3/4" sq. (B6)
• Fourteen – 1 1/4" wide strips. From these, cut:
   * Two – 1 1/4" x 42" (inner side borders)
   * Four – 1 1/4" x 39 1/2" (inner top and bottom borders) Piece two together to = 78 1/2" length. Make 2.
   * Four – 1 1/4" x 30 3/4" (inner side borders) Add to opposite short ends of 42" long strip to = 102 1/2" long border. Make 2.
   * Forty-eight – 1 1/4" x 2" (A4)
   * Forty-eight – 1 1/4" sq. (A5b)

From Fabric IV, cut: (medium green print)
• Two 3 1/4" wide strips. From these, cut:
   * Forty-eight – 1 3/4" x 3 1/4" (A10)
• Eight 2 3/4" wide strips. From these, cut:
   * Ninety-six – 2 3/4" x 3 1/8" (A2, A13)
• Two 2" wide strips. From these, cut:
   * Forty-eight – 1 3/4" x 2" (A8)
• Seven 1 3/4" wide strips. From these, cut:
   * Ninety-six – 1 3/4" sq. (B2)
   * Forty-eight – 1 1/8" x 1 3/4" (A12a)
• Seven 1 1/4" wide strips. Four for Strip Set 1.
From remaining three strips, cut:
   * Ninety-six – 1 1/4" sq. (A6)
• Four 1 1/8" wide strips. From these, cut:
   * 144 – 1 1/8" sq. (A11a, B4a)

From Fabric V, cut: (white on white print)
• Three 19" wide strips. From these, cut:
   * Six – 19" sq. (setting squares for embroidery) Cut down to 18 1/2" square when embroidery is completed.
• From scrap, cut:

- One 2 3/4" wide strip. From this, cut:
  * Twelve – 2" x 2 3/4" (add to A5)
- Eight 2 1/2" wide strips. From these, cut:
  * 192 – 1 3/4" x 2 1/2" (B1, B4)
- Six 1 1/8" wide strips. From these, cut:
  * 192 – 1 1/8" squares (B3a)

From Fabric VI, cut: (medium gold print)
- Three 2 1/2" wide strips. From these, cut:
  * Forty-eight – 2 1/2" sq. (B3)

ASSEMBLY

Making The Rose Block
Block A
1. The entire rose block is divided into two blocks; Block A, and Block B. These blocks are joined after they are completed to make the Rose Block shown on page 72. Refer to Block A diagram frequently for correct placement of all units.

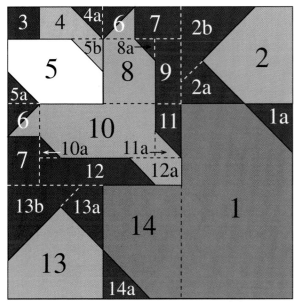

Block A - Make 48. Finishes to 6 3/4" square

2. Use diagonal corner technique to make one each of units 1, 2, 4, 5, 8, 10, 11, 13, and 14. For diagonal corner units 2 and 13, take care to join the corners in alphabetical order, as one is smaller than the other.

3. Use diagonal end technique to make one of Unit 12. See illustration below for assembly of this unit. Use triangle-square technique to make two of Unit 6. Refer to illustration above right, on how to make this unit.

Making Unit 12 for Block A

4. To assemble the block, begin by joining units 1 and 2. Join units 3 and 4; then join Unit 5 to bottom of combined 3-4 units. Refer to diagram for correct placement of the following units: Join one each of units 6 and 7. Join unit 8 and 9. Join the correct combined 6-7 units to top of the 8-9 combined units as shown, matching seams. Add this combination to right side of combined units 3-5.

5. Join remaining units 6 and 7. Join units 10 and 11; then add Unit 12 to bottom of combined 10-11 units. Join the combined 6-7 units to left side as shown. Add these combined units to the bottom of the bud. Join units 13 and 14; then add to bottom of bud. Join the combined 1-2 units, to the right side of the bud to complete the block.

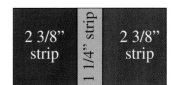

Use this assembly for Block A, Unit 6

Place 1 1/4" squares of fabrics I and IV right sides together, matching raw edges, and stitch a diagonal line down the center as shown. Press open and trim center seam, leaving the top and base fabric.

Use this assembly for Block B, Unit 2

Place 1 3/4" squares of fabrics I and IV right sides together, matching raw edges, and stitch a diagonal line down the center as shown. Press open and trim center seam, leaving the top and base fabric.

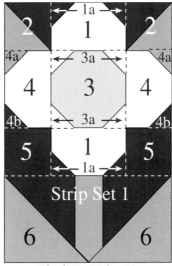

Block B - Make 48.
Finishes to 4 1/2" x 6 3/4"

Strip Set 1. Make 4.
Cut into 48 - 2 3/4" segments

Making Block B
1. To make Block B, first assemble the strip set as shown above. Follow instructions given and cut into segments.
2. Use diagonal corner technique to make two each of units 1 and 4. Make one of Unit 3. Refer to instructions given in gold box above for making triangle-square Unit 2. Make 96 of these units.
3. To assemble the block, refer to the block diagram for correct placement of Unit 2 and begin by joining units 2-1- and 2 in a horizontal row. Join units 4-3-4 in a horizontal row. Join units 5-1-5 in a row as shown. Join the three rows together, matching corner seams. Join diagonal corner Unit 6 to each side to Strip Set 1 segment as shown, trimming and pressing. Add this unit to bottom of flower to complete Block B.

Completing The Rose Block
1. Refer to illustration of Rose Block on next page. Beginning at the top, join blocks A-B-and A in a row as shown. Make two of these rows. Join Block B, Unit Q1 And Block B in a row which will be used as the center row. Refer to the illustration, and join the three rows to complete the Rose Block. Make 12.

Embroidery Placement
1. Follow directions given in the cutting instructions for cutting the correct sizes of the squares to be used for the embroideries. Illustrations have been given to show the exact placement of the embroideries. If you wish to make the quilt without the embroideries, the quilting designs are also provided for you. We suggest quilting the designs (with or without the embroideries) in a pink colored thread on the white squares, and an ivory colored thread on the medium rose squares so the quilting stands out. When embroidery is complete cut the squares into triangles as shown. The white on white setting squares are embroidered in the center; then pressed and cut down to 18 1/2" squares.

Block A   Block B   Block A

Rose Block. Make 12. Finishes to 18" square.

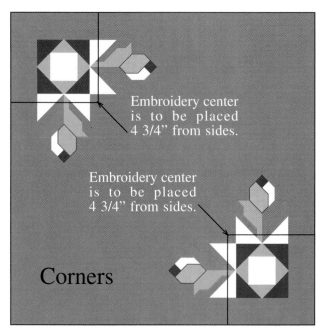

Embroidery center is to be placed 4 3/4" from sides.

Embroidery center is to be placed 4 3/4" from sides.

Corners

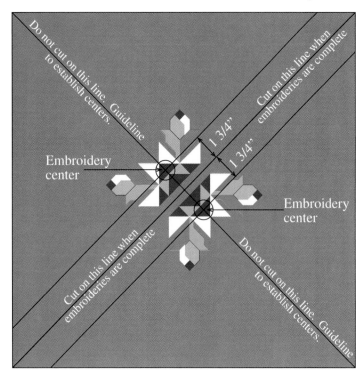

Do not cut on this line. Guideline to establish centers.

Cut on this line when embroideries are complete

1 3/4"
1 3/4"

Embroidery center

Embroidery center

Cut on this line when embroideries are complete

Do not cut on this line. Guideline to establish centers.

Embroidery placement for large border triangles.

Trim off 2" around outer edge of square

Cut in half diagonally

Embroidery placement for corner triangles.

Quilt Assembly

1. Refer to illustration on page 73. Square and triangular blocks are assembled with the square blocks "on point." Begin in the top left hand corner and join a corner triangle to a Rose Block as shown. For the first row, join large triangle, Rose Block and another large triangle, forming the top right corner. Make two of these. One for Row 1, and one for Row 6. Refer to quilt diagram for correct placement of triangles. For Row 2, join a large triangle, Rose Block, Setting Square, Rose Block and another large triangle. Make two of these rows, the second for Row 5.

2. The quilt top may be assembled as you desire. You can mark the rows and wait until they are all complete or you may join them as you go along. We like to join as we go along.

3. For rows 3 and 4, join one large triangle to Rose Block, then a setting square, another Rose Block, setting square, one more Rose Block, and a large triangle.

4. Join the rows together as shown. Add long outer side borders first; then join top and bottom outer borders to complete the top.

Pillow. Finishes to 16" square

Finishes to 82" x 107 1/2"

MATERIALS FOR PILLOWCASES (Set of 2)
Fabric I (dark burgundy print) Need 1 1/4" 1/8 yard
Fabric II (medium rose print) Need 10 3/4" 3/8 yard
Fabric III (medium green print) Need 6 1/2" 1/4 yard
Fabric IV (white on white print) Need 73 1/2" 2 1/8 yards
Fabric V (medium gold print) Need 2 1/2" 1/8 yard

CUTTING

From Fabric I, cut: (dark burgundy print)
• Two 1 1/4" wide strips. From these, cut:
  * Two – 1 1/4" x 40 1/2" (Q2)

From Fabric II, cut: (medium rose print)
• One 3 1/4" wide strip. From this, cut:
  * Sixteen – 2 1/2" x 3 1/4" (C7)
• One 2" wide strip. From this, cut:
  * Sixteen – 2" sq. (C6a)
• Two 1 3/4" wide strips. From these, cut:
  * Thirty-two – 1 3/4" sq. (C2, C5)
  * Sixteen – 1 1/2" sq. (C6b)
• Two 1" wide strips. From these, cut:
  * Forty-eight – 1" sq. (C3a, C4b)

From Fabric III, cut: (medium green print)
• Two 3 1/4" wide strips. From these, cut:
  * Sixteen – 3" x 3 1/4" (C6)
  * Sixteen – 1" sq. (C4a)
  * Sixteen – 1 3/4" sq. (C2)

From Fabric IV, cut: (white on white print)
• Two 20 1/2" wide strips. From these, cut:
  * Two – 20 1/2" x 40 1/2" sq. (Q1)
• Two 13 3/4" wide strips. From these, cut:
  * Two – 13 3/4" x 40 1/2" (Q3)
• Two 2 1/2" wide strips. From these, cut:
  * Thirty-two – 1 3/4" x 2 1/2" (C3, C4)
  * Thirty-two – 1 1/8" sq. (C1a)

From Fabric V, cut: (medium gold print)
• One 2 1/2" wide strip. From this, cut:
  * Eight – 2 1/2" squares (C1)

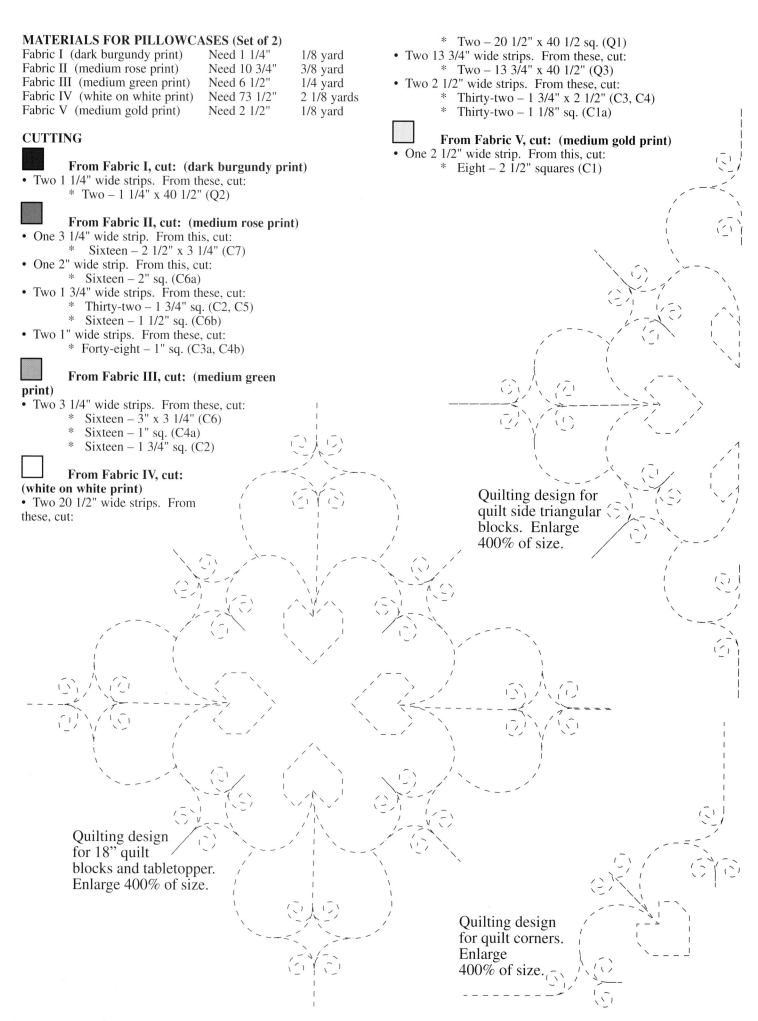

Quilting design for quilt side triangular blocks. Enlarge 400% of size.

Quilting design for 18" quilt blocks and tabletopper. Enlarge 400% of size.

Quilting design for quilt corners. Enlarge 400% of size.

74

MATERIALS FOR TABLE TOPPER

■	Fabric I (dark burgundy print)	Need 13 3/4"	1/2 yard
■	Fabric II (medium rose print)	Need 14 1/2"	1/2 yard
■	Fabric IV (medium green print)	Need 6 1/2"	1/4 yard
□	Fabric V (white on white print)	Need 39 1/2"	1 1/4 yards
□	Fabric VI (medium gold print)	Need 2 1/2"	1/8 yard
	Backing		1 1/4 yards

CUTTING FOR TABLE TOPPER

■ **From Fabric I, cut: (dark burgundy print)**
• Four – 2 1/2" wide strips for straight-grain binding.
• Three – 1 1/4" wide strips. From this, cut:
  * Four – 1 1/4" x 20 1/2" (center frame)
  * Eight – 1 1/4" sq. (Q1a, Q4b)

■ **From Fabric II, cut: (medium rose print)**
• One 5 3/4" wide strip. From this, cut:
  * Four – 5 3/4" sq. (Q4a)
  * Sixteen – 1 1/2" sq. (C6b)
  * Forty-eight – 1" sq. (C3a, C4b)
• One 3 1/4" wide strip. From this, cut:
  * Sixteen – 2 1/2" x 3 1/4" (C7)
• One 2" wide strip. From this, cut:
  * Sixteen – 2" sq. (C6a)
• Two 1 3/4" wide strips. From these, cut:
  * Thirty-two – 1 3/4" sq. (C2, C5)

■ **From Fabric III, cut: (medium green print)**
• Two 3 1/4" wide strips. From these, cut:
  * Sixteen – 3" x 3 1/4" (C6)
  * Sixteen – 1" sq. (C4a)
  * Sixteen – 1 3/4" sq. (C2)

□ **From Fabric IV, cut: (white on white print)**
• One 22 1/2" wide strip. From this, cut:
  * One – 22 1/2" sq. (Q1) Complete embroidery and press. Trim to 20 1/2" square.
  * Two – 7" x 20 1/2" (Q3) After unit is added to Block C borders, stitch embroideries and decorative quilting lines; then trim to 3" width.
• One 8 7/8" wide strip. From this, cut:
  * Two – 8 7/8" sq. (Q4)
  * One - 7" x 20 1/2" (add to Q3)
• One 7" wide strip. From this, cut:
  * One - 7" x 20 1/2" (add to Q3)
  * Thirty-two – 1 3/4" x 2 1/2" (C3, C4)
• One 1 1/8" wide strip. From this, cut:
  * Thirty-two – 1 1/8" sq. (C1a)

□ **From Fabric V, cut: (medium gold print)**
• One 2 1/2" wide strip. From this, cut:
  * Eight – 2 1/2" squares (C1).

ASSEMBLY

Block C Assembly
1. Refer to illustration below, and use diagonal corner technique to make two each of units 3, 4, and 6. Make one of Unit 1. Refer to our illustration of triangle-square Unit 2, and make 16. Be sure to join diagonal corners for Unit 6 in alphabetical order.

Use this assembly for Block C, Unit 2

Place 1 3/4" squares of fabrics II and III right sides together, matching raw edges, and stitch a diagonal line down the center as shown. Press open and trim center seam, leaving the top and base fabric.

2. To assemble the block, begin by joining units 2-3-2 in a horizontal row. Join units 4-1-4 in a row. Join units 5-3-5 in a row. Join the three rows together, matching corner seams.
3. Join units 6 and 7, referring to illustration for correct placement of mirror image units. Add these combined units to opposite sides of the flower to complete the block. Make 8.

Table topper Assembly
1. Stitch the embroidery first for the center section (Q1). Trim it down to a 20 1/2" square; then add diagonal corners Q1a as shown. Join two of Block C as shown on table topper illustration on page 76. Add the 7" x 20 1/2" piece (Q3) across the bottom. Embroidery will be stitched so that point of center rose is 3/4" from where leaves meet. When embroidery is completed, remove from

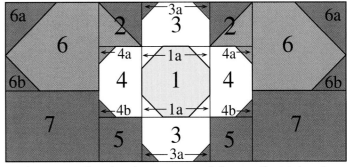

Section C. Finishes to 4 1/2" x 10". Make 8 for tabletopper and 4 for each pillowcase.

Finishes to:
36" square

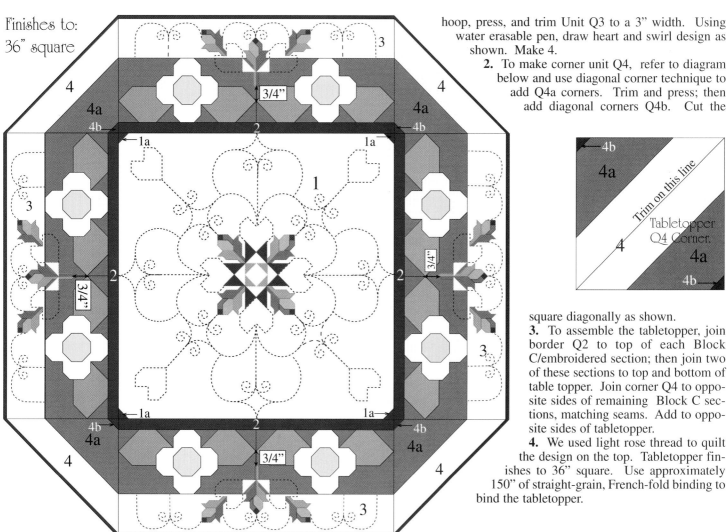

hoop, press, and trim Unit Q3 to a 3" width. Using water erasable pen, draw heart and swirl design as shown. Make 4.

2. To make corner unit Q4, refer to diagram below and use diagonal corner technique to add Q4a corners. Trim and press; then add diagonal corners Q4b. Cut the

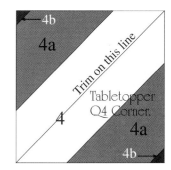

square diagonally as shown.

3. To assemble the tabletopper, join border Q2 to top of each Block C/embroidered section; then join two of these sections to top and bottom of table topper. Join corner Q4 to opposite sides of remaining Block C sections, matching seams. Add to opposite sides of tabletopper.

4. We used light rose thread to quilt the design on the top. Tabletopper finishes to 36" square. Use approximately 150" of straight-grain, French-fold binding to bind the tabletopper.

Making The Pillowcases
Cutting instructions and yardage requirements are on page 74.

1. Refer to illustrations and instructions for Block C on page 75. Make four of Block C for each pillowcase. Join in a horizontal row as shown. Join Unit Q3 to bottom and stitch embroidereries as for tabletopper.

2. To assemble, refer to pillowcase diagram at right and begin by joining Unit Q2 to top of flowers, and Unit Q1 to top of Unit Q2.

3. Fold the pillowcase in half, right sides together, and serge or use overcast stitch around 2 sides, leaving bottom open. Turn right side out and press under 1/4" hem. Press the lining up inside, about 4" below the floral border. Turn pillowcase wrong side out, and whip stitch the lining in place. Lining should cover raw seams of border.

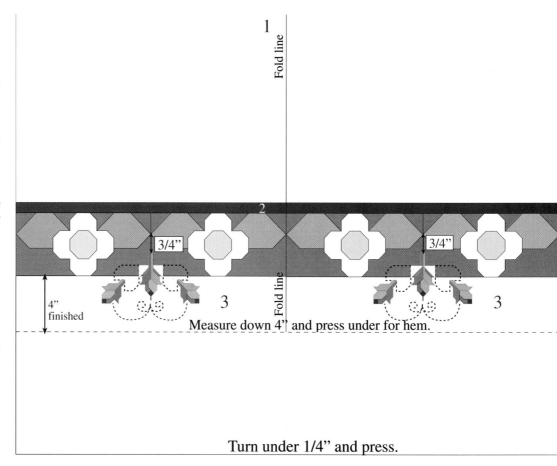

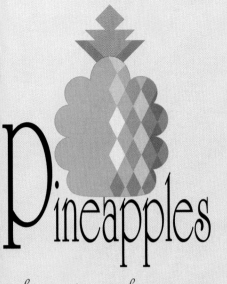

Pineapples

There is a lot to be said for smaller projects when you are in need of a special gift that can be made in a relatively short period of time. Nothing says it better than Pineapples, which are traditionally referred to as the "Welcome" sign.

In this case we have given the pineapple designs a country feeling by the fabrics we have selected, and simple frayed napkins next to the place mats.

The setting in which the two placemats are shown gives a casual, yet tasteful atmosphere. Living and natural things add charm to any table. In the home decor shopping category, keep in mind your local thrift shops. Gigi found the brass pineapple at the thrift store for .50 cents! It was tarnished, but hey, a little brass cleaner and elbow grease can work wonders!

Welcome sign finishes to: 28" square.
Table runner finishes to: 22 1/2" x 30 1/2"
Place mat finishes to: 14" x 19 1/2"
Welcome sign Block A finishes to 7 1/2" square
All other blocks finish to: 5 1/2" x 9"

MATERIALS FOR WELCOME SIGN

	Fabric I (light tan print)	Need 20 7/8"	5/8 yard
	Fabric II (dark green print)	Need 18 7/8"	5/8 yard
	Fabric III (light green print)	Need 2 3/4"	1/8 yard
	Fabric IV (medium barn red print)	Need 4"	1/4 yard
	Fabric V (dark barn red print)	Need 4"	1/4 yard
	Fabric VI (gold print)	Need 6 1/2"s sq.	Scrap
	Backing		1 yard

Techniques used: Diagonal Corners and Diagonal Ends.

Welcome

CUTTING FOR WELCOME SIGN

From Fabric I, cut: (light tan print)
- One 2 7/8" wide strip. From this, cut:
  * Four - 2 7/8" sq. (A14)
  * Eight – 2" x 2 3/8" (A1, A8)
  * Eight – 1 3/8" x 2" (A11a)
- Five 2" wide strips. From these, cut:
  * Four – 2" x 15 3/4" (Q3, Q4)
  * Four – 2" x 5 5/8" (Q8a)
  * Eight – 2" x 4 3/8" (A12)
  * Four – 2" x 4 1/8" (Q6a)
  * Sixteen – 2" sq. (Q5a, Q6b, Q7a, Q8b)
  * Two – 1" x 24 1/2" (Q10)
- One 1 3/4" wide strip. From this, cut:
  * Twelve – 1 3/4" sq. (Q4b, A13a)
- Two 1 1/2" wide strips. From these, cut:
  * Two – 1 1/2" x 17 1/2" (Q2)
  * Two – 1 1/2" x 15 1/2" (Q1)
- One 1 1/4" wide strip. From this, cut:
  * Eight – 1 1/4" sq. (A9b, A10b)
  * Sixteen – 1 1/8" sq. (A2a, A4a, A6a, A7a)
- Two 1" wide strips. From these, cut:
  * Two – 1" x 23 1/2" (Q9)

From Fabric II, cut: (dark green print)
- Seven 2 1/2" wide strips. Three strips for straight-grain binding. From remaining four, cut:
  * Two – 2 1/2" x 28 1/2" (Q12)
  * Two – 2 1/2" x 24 1/2" (Q11)
  * Eight – 1 5/8" x 2 3/8" (A9a, A10a)
  * Eight – 1 3/4" x 2 7/8" (A13)
  * Four – 1 3/8" sq. (A14a)
  * Eight – 1 1/8" sq. (A11b)
- One 1 3/8" wide strip. From this, cut:
  * Eight – 1 3/8" x 3 3/4" (A11)

From Fabric III , cut: (light green print)
- One 1 5/8" wide strip. From this, cut:
  * Four – 1 5/8" x 4 7/8" (A10)
  * Four – 1 5/8" x 3 3/4" (A9)
  * Four – 1 3/8" sq. (A5)

- One 1 1/8" wide strip. From this, cut:
  * Four – 1 1/8" x 2 5/8" (A4)
  * Four – 1 1/8" x 2" (A2)
  * Eight – 1 1/8" x 1 3/8" (A6, A7)
  * Four – 1 1/8" sq. (A3a)

From Fabric IV, cut: (medium barn red print)
- Two 2" wide strips. From these, cut:
  * Four – 2" x 5 5/8" (Q5, Q7)
  * Four – 2" x 4 3/8" (Q4a)
  * Four – 2" x 2 7/8" (Q3a)

From Fabric V, cut: (dark barn red check)
- Two 2" wide strips. From these, cut:
  * Eight – 2" x 5 5/8" (Q6, Q8)

From Fabric VI, cut: (gold print)
- Four 3" squares (A3)

ASSEMBLY

Making Block A

1. Use diagonal corner technique to make two of Unit 13. Make one each of units 2, 3, 4, 6, 7, and 14.

2. Use diagonal end technique to make two mirror image Unit 11, and one each of units 9, and 10. Illustrations below show how to piece these units properly.

3. To assemble Block A, begin by joining units 1 and 2; then add Unit 3 to bottom of combined units. Join units 5, 6, 7, in a vertical row. Join Unit 4 to right side of these combined units.

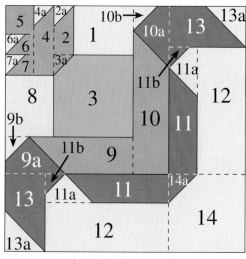

Block A. Make 4.

Join Unit 8 to bottom. Add 4-8 combined units to combined units 1-3 as shown.

4. Join Unit 9 to bottom of pineapple combined units;

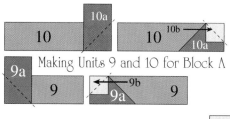

Making Units 9 and 10 for Block A

then join Unit 10 to side. Refer to block diagram for correct placement of mirror image

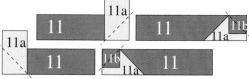

Making mirror image units 11 for Block A

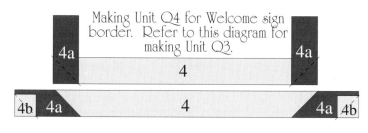

Making Unit Q4 for Welcome sign border. Refer to this diagram for making Unit Q3.

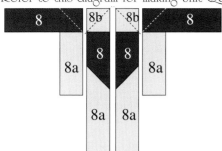

Making Unit Q8 for Welcome sign border.
Refer to this diagram for making Unit Q6.

units 11 and 13. Join units 11 and 12; then add Unit 13 to these combined units. Join to right side of Pineapple as shown. Add Unit 14 to remaining combined units 11-13 and add to bottom of pineapple to complete the block. Make 4. Join the four pineapples together as shown.

Assembling The Sign

1. Refer to diagram of the sign at right. Join Unit Q1 to top and bottom of sign; then add Unit Q2 to opposite sides.

2. Use diagonal corner technique to make two each of units Q5 and Q7. Use diagonal end technique to make four each of units Q6 and and Q8. Use this technique to make two each of units Q3 and Q4. Refer to the illustration at the bottom of page 78 and above for construction of these units.

3. Join Unit Q3 to top and bottom of sign; then join Unit Q4 to opposite sides. Join mirror image Unit Q6 to opposite sides of Unit Q5. Make two and join to top and bottom of sign. Join mirror image Unit Q8 to opposite sides of Unit Q7 as shown. Join to opposite sides of sign. Add Unit Q9 to top and bottom; then join Unit Q10 to sides. Join Unit Q11 to top and bottom; then add Unit Q12 to sides to complete the sign.

4. We added our favorite font to the center for the word "Welcome." The quilting was very simple. "Ditch" all of the patchwork. Use approximately 120" of straight-grain, French-fold binding to bind the edges. It is desirable to make a hanging sleeve for the back.

MATERIALS FOR TABLE RUNNER

	Fabric I (light tan print)	Need 6 1/2"	1/4 yard
	Fabric II (med. brown batik)	Need 7"	1/4 yard
	Fabric III (pale gold print)	Need 4 1/8"	1/4 yard
	Fabric IV (gold print)	Need 4 1/8"	1/4 yard
	Fabric V (light gold print)	Need 7 1/8"	3/8 yard
	Fabric VI (med. gold print)	Need 4 1/8"	1/4 yard
	Fabric VII (med. green print)	Need 6 1/2"	1/4 yard
	Fabric VIII (dk. green check)	Need 19"	5/8 yard
	Fabric IX (dark brown print)	Need 10 1/8"	3/8 yard
	Backing		3/4 yard

CUTTING FOR TABLE RUNNER

From Fabric I, cut: (light tan print)
- One 2 5/8" wide strip. From this, cut:
  * Eight – 2 5/8" sq. (A6b)
  * Eight – 2" x 2 1/4" (A5)
- One 2 3/8" strip. From this, cut:
  * Eight – 2 3/8" sq. (A1a)
  * Eight – 1 5/8" x 2 3/8" (A2a)
  * Eight – 1" sq. (A4b)
- One 1 1/2" wide strip. From this, cut:
  * Eight – 1 1/2" sq. (A4a)
  * Eight – 1" x 2 1/4" (A3a)

From Fabric II, cut: (medium brown batik)
- One 2 5/8" wide strip. From this, cut:
  * Eight – 2 5/8" sq. (B6b)
  * Eight – 1" x 2 1/4" (B3a)
  * Two – 2" x 6" (Q3)
- One 2 3/8" strip. From this, cut:
  * Eight – 2 3/8" sq. (B1a)
  * Eight – 1 5/8" x 2 3/8" (B2a)
  * Eight – 1" sq. (B4b)
- One 2" wide strip. From this, cut:
  * Eight – 2" x 2 1/4" (B5)
  * Eight – 1 1/2" sq. (B4a)

From Fabric III, cut: (pale gold print)
- One 2 5/8" wide strip. From this, cut:
  * Four – 2 5/8" sq. (C6b)
  * Four – 2 3/8" sq. (C1a)
  * Four – 1 5/8" x 2 3/8" (C2a)
  * Four – 2" x 2 1/4" (C5)
  * Four – 1" x 2 1/4" (C3a)
- One 1 1/2" wide strip. From this, cut:
  * Four – 1 1/2" sq. (C4a)
  * Four – 1" sq. (C4b)

From Fabric IV, cut: (dark gold diamond print)
- One 4 1/8" wide strip. From this, cut:
  * Two - 4 1/8" x 6" (C1)

From Fabric V, cut: (light gold print)
- One 4 1/8" wide strip. From this, cut:
  * Four – 4 1/8" x 6" (B1)
- Three 1" wide strips. From these, cut:
  * Two – 1" x 28" (Q4)
  * Two – 1" x 21" (Q5)

From Fabric VI, cut: (medium gold print)
- One 4 1/8" wide strip. From this, cut:
  * Four – 4 1/8" x 6" (A1)

From Fabric VII, cut: (medium green print)
- One 4 1/2" wide strip. From this, cut:
  * Two – 1 5/8" x 4 1/2" (C2)
  * Two – 1" x 3 1/2" (C3)
  * Twelve – 2 3/4" x 3 1/4" (A6, C6)
- One 2" wide strip. From this, cut:
  * Two – 2" x 6" (Q2)
  * Two – 2" x 2 1/2" (C4)
  * Twelve – 1 3/4" sq. (A1c, C1c)

From Fabric VIII, cut: (dark green check)
- One 3 1/2" wide strip. From this, cut:
  * Eight – 2 3/4" x 3 1/4" (B6)
  * Four – 1" x 3 1/2" (B3)
  * One – 2" x 6" (Q1)
  * Eight – 1 3/4" sq. (B1c)

- Three 2 1/2" wide strips for straight-grain binding
- One 2" wide strip. From this, cut:
  * Four – 2" x 2 1/2" (B4)
  * Four – 1 5/8" x 4 1/2" (B2)
- Four 1 1/2" wide strips. From these, cut:
  * Two – 1 1/2" x 29" (Q6)
  * Two – 1 1/2" x 23" (Q7)

From Fabric IX, cut: (dark brown print)
- Two 3 1/4" wide strips. From these, cut:
  * Twenty – 3 1/4" sq. (A1b, B1b, C1b)
  * Four – 2" x 2 1/2" (A4)
  * Four – 1" x 3 1/2" (A3)
- One 2" wide strip. From this, cut:
  * Twenty – 2" sq. (A6a, B6a, C6a)
- One 1 5/8" wide strip. From this, cut:
  * Four – 1 5/8" x 4 1/2" (A2)

Assembly

Although this table runner is shown on our antique ice box, it makes a delightful center for any table. Using the place mats with it is an added plus as all of the colors work nicely together.

Making The Pineapple Blocks
1. All of the pineapple blocks are constructed in the same way.
2. Use diagonal corner technique to make two of mirror image Unit 6. Use this technique to make one each of units 1, and 4. When making diagonal corners on units 1 and 6, keep in mind to add them in alphabetical order.
3. Use diagonal end technique to make one each of units 2 and 3. Construction for units 2 and 3 are the same, illustrated at right.
4. To assemble the blocks, join units 1, 2, and 3 in a row. Join units 5-4-5 in a horizontal row and add to top of combined units 1-3. Join the two mirror image Units 6, matching seams;

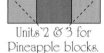

Units 2 & 3 for Pineapple blocks.

then add them to the bottom of the pineapple, again matching seams.

Table runner Assembly
1. Refer to the table runner diagram on the next page, and begin assembly by joining pineapple blocks A, B, C, B and A in a hori-

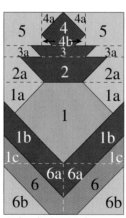 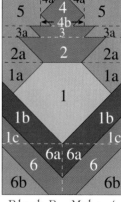

Block A Make 4.   Block B. Make 4.   Block C. Make 2.

zontal row. Make two rows.
2. Join units Q3, Q2, Q1, Q2, and Q3 in a horizontal row. Refer once again to the diagram and join the pineapple rows to opposite long sides of the Q1-Q3 units. Press seams towards center. Join Unit Q4 to top and bottom of table runner; then add Unit Q5 to opposite sides. Join Unit Q6 to top and bottom of table runner; then add Unit Q7 to opposite sides to complete the table runner.
3. The pineapples were quilted with a cross-hatch grid, and all patchwork was "ditched." We used approximately 115" of straight-grain, French-fold binding to bind the edge.

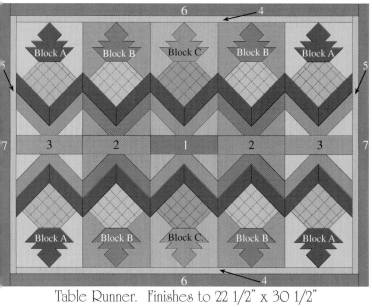

Table Runner. Finishes to 22 1/2" x 30 1/2"

MATERIALS FOR PLACE MATS

☐	Fabric I (light tan print)	Need 14 1/2"	3/8 yard
▨	Fabric II (med. gold print)	Need 3 5/8"	1/4 yard
▨	Fabric III (lt. gold print)		Lg. scrap
▨	Fabric IV (med. brown batik)		Lg. scrap
▨	Fabric V (med. green print)	Need 6"	1/4 yard
▨	Fabric VI (dk. green check)	Need 2 3/8"	1/8 yard
■	Fabric VII (dk. red check)	Need 23 3/4"	3/4 yard
	Backing for 2 place mats		1/2 yard

CUTTING FOR PLACE MATS

From Fabric I, cut: (light tan print)
- One 14 1/2" wide strip. From this, cut:
  * Two – 9 1/2" x 14 1/2" (Q1)
  * Two – 1" x 11 3/4" (Q2)
  * Ten – 2 3/4" sq. (Q3a)
  * Ten – 2 1/8" sq. (Q3c)
  * Two – 3 1/4" sq. (Q4a)
  * Two – 2 5/8" sq. (Q4c)

From Fabric II, cut: (medium gold print)
- One 2 5/8" wide strip. From this, cut:
  * Four – 2 5/8" sq. (A6b)
  * Four – 2 3/8" sq. (A1a)
  * Four – 1 5/8" x 2 3/8" (A2a)
  * Four – 2" x 2 1/4" (A5)
  * Four – 1 1/2" sq. (A4a)
- One 1" wide strip. From this, cut:
  * Four – 1" x 2 1/4" (A3a)
  * Four – 1" sq. (A4b)

From Fabric III, cut: (light gold print)
- Two – 4 1/8" x 6" (A1)

From Fabric IV, cut: (medium brown batik)
- Two – 1 3/4" x 6" (Q7)

From Fabric V, cut: (medium green print)
- One 3 1/4" wide strip. From this, cut:
  * Two – 3 1/4" x 4" (Q4b)
  * Four – 2 3/4" x 3 1/4" (A6)
  * Two – 2 3/8" x 6" (Q6)
  * Four – 1 3/4" sq. (A1c)
- One 2 3/4" wide strip. From this, cut:
  * Ten – 2 3/4" x 3 1/2" (Q3b)

From Fabric VI, cut: (dark green check)
- One 2 3/8" wide strip. From this, cut:
  * Two – 2 3/8" x 6" (Q5)
  * Two – 2" x 2 1/2" (A4)
  * Two – 1 5/8" x 4 1/2" (A2)
  * Two - 1" x 3 1/2" (A3)

From Fabric VII, cut: (dark barn red check)
- One 12 1/2" wide strip. From this, cut:
  * Two – 12 1/2" squares for napkins
  * Ten – 2 3/4" x 4 1/4" (Q3)
  * Two – 3 1/4" x 4 3/4" (Q4)
- Four 2" wide strips for straight-grain binding
- One 3 1/4" wide strip. From this, cut:
  * Four – 3 1/4" sq. (A1b)
  * Four – 2" sq. (A6a)

Assembly

Place mat Assembly - Block A

1. Refer to diagrams and Steps 1-4 for Making The Pineapple Blocks on page 80. Make two of Block A at right.
2. Refer to illustration of place mat above, and use diagonal end technique to make five of mirror image Unit Q3. Make one of Unit Q4. Follow diagram, and add all diagonal ends and corners in alphabetical order.

82

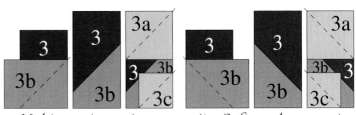

Making mirror image units 3 for place mat. Refer to this diagram to make Unit 4.

Assembling The Place mat

1. To assemble the place mat, begin by joining mirror image units Q3 as shown, making sure to take care in matching seams. Join Unit Q2 along top of Unit Q3 row; then add Unit Q4 to right side as shown. Join Unit Q1 to top of combined lower units.

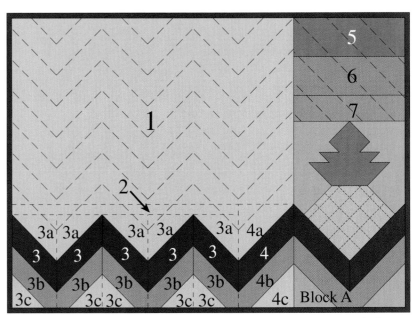

Place mat finishes to 14" x 19 1/2"

2. Join units Q5, Q6, Q7, and Block A in a vertical row as shown; then add to right side of place mat.
3. Once again, we did cross-hatch quilting in the pineapple, and a shadow quilting on the place mat as shown. We used approximately 145" of straight-grain, French-fold binding to bind the edges.
4. Napkins were top stitched 1/2" from edge and then frayed. We found a nice woven cotton for the dark red for ease in fraying the edges. The napkins give a nice, warm, country feeling.

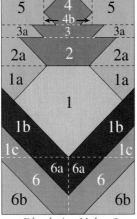

Block A. Make 2

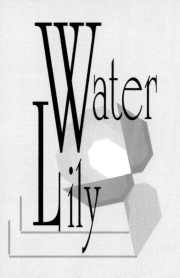

Water Lily

Robert and I were born and raised in St Louis, Missouri. Before we moved to Colorado, we lived in a wonderful historic Victorian home. We especially loved and appreciated the craftsmanship of a time when great pride was taken in the workmanship of a home and its furnishings.

Pocket doors were throughout the house, impeccable parquet flooring, and wanes coating in the parlor and dining room.

We wanted a quilt design that would lend itself to a beautiful Victorian bedroom. When the Water Lily quilt was completed, and the embroideries added, we were compelled to embroider a coordinating dresser scarf on Belgian linen to further capture the ambiance of a truly elegant period in history.

A lovely Jinny Beyer floral print was my first choice. When it was time to do the pillowcases, I decided to utilize the print once again, picking up a touch of the gold linen, and emphasizing the embroideries on the pillowcase borders.

Faye enhanced our design once again with her creative quilting, adding to the feeling by stitching a feathery motif on the borders of the quilt using a light tan thread on the darker border.

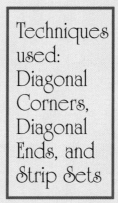

Quilt finishes to: 78" x 95 1/2".
Blocks A and B finish to 9 1/2" square.
Dresser scarf finishes to: 26" x 39 1/4 from tip to tip.

Techniques used: Diagonal Corners, Diagonal Ends, and Strip Sets

MATERIALS FOR QUILT

☐	Fabric I (ivory print)	Need 175"	5 yards
▦	Fabric II (floral teal and tan print)	Need 33 1/8"	1 yard
▦	Fabric III (dark teal print)	Need 97 1/8"	2 5/8 yards
▦	Fabric IV (medium teal print)	Need 50"	1 1/2 yards
▦	Fabric V (honey tan print)	Need 34 1/4"	1 1/8 yards
▦	Fabric VI (med mint green print)	Need 55"	1 5/8 yards
▦	Fabric VII (light mint print)	Need 54 1/8"	1 5/8 yards
	Backing		5 3/4 yards

For Quilt and Pillowcase Embroideries:

Robison Anton #40 weight rayon embroidery thread: #2335 Ivory, #2492 Turquoise, #2312 Isle Green, #2318 Pale Green, #2735 Pro Green, and #2630 Pro Beige.

CUTTING FOR QUILT

From Fabric I, cut: (ivory print)
- Six 4 3/8" wide strips. From these, cut:
  * Forty-eight – 4 3/8" sq. (A19)
- Fourteen 3 1/8" wide strips. From these, cut:
  * Ninety-six – 3 1/8" sq. (A18)
  * 160 – 1 5/8" x 3 1/8" (A13, B13)
- Sixteen 3" wide strips. From these, cut:
  * 160 – 3" sq. (A15, B15)
  * 160 – 1 1/8" x 2 7/8" (A16, B16)
- Five 2 5/8" wide strips. From these, cut:
  * Eighty - 2 5/8" sq. (A1, B1)
- Seven 1 3/4" wide strips. From these, cut:
  * 160 – 1 3/4" sq. (A7a, B7a)
- Four 1 1/2" wide strips. From these, cut:
  * 160 – 7/8" x 1 1/2" (A4, B4)
- Six 1 3/8" wide strips. From these and scrap, cut:
  * 160 – 1 3/8" sq. (A14a, B14a)
- Eight 1 1/4" wide strips. From these, cut:
  * 240 – 1 1/4" sq. (A2a, A6, B2a, B6)
- Three 1 1/8" wide strips. From these, cut:
  * Eighty – 1 1/8" sq. (A8, B8)
- Four 1" wide strips. From these, cut:
  * 160 – 1" sq. (A11b, B11b)

From Fabric II, cut: (floral teal and tan print)
- Four 4 3/8" wide strips. From these, cut:
  * Thirty-two – 4 3/8" sq. (B19)
- Five 3 1/8" wide strips. From these, cut:
  * Sixty-four – 3 1/8" sq. (B18)

From Fabric III, cut: (dark teal print)
- Seven – 4 3/8" wide strips. From these, cut:
  * 160 – 1 3/4" x 4 3/8" (A7, B7)
- Ten 3 1/2" wide strips. From these, cut:
  * Two – 3 1/2" x 42" (side quilt borders)
  * Four – 3 1/2" x 24 3/4" (side borders) Piece the 24 3/4" cuts on opposite sides of the 42" strip to make two 90 1/2" lengths.
  * Four – 3 1/2" x 39 1/2" (top and bottom quilt borders) Piece two together to make two 78 1/2" lengths.
- Nine 2 1/2" wide strips for straight-grain binding.
- Four 2 1/4" wide strips. From these, cut:
  * Sixty-four – 2 1/4" sq. (B11)

From Fabric IV, cut: (medium teal print)
- Twelve 2 1/4" wide strips. From these, cut:
  * 96 – 2 1/4" sq. (A11)
  * 160 – 1 1/2" x 2 1/4" (A2, B2)
- Six 1 1/2" wide strips. From these, cut:
  * . Eighty – 1 1/2" x 1 7/8" (A3, B3)
  * Eighty – 7/8" x 1 1/2" (A5, B5)
- Seven 1 1/4" wide strips for Strip Set 1
- Six 7/8" wide strips. From these, cut:
  * 240 – 7/8" sq. (A4a, A6a, B4a, B6a)

From Fabric V, cut: (honey tan print)
- Sixteen 1 1/2" wide strips. Seven strips for Strip Set 1. From remaining 9 strips, cut:
  * 240 – 1 1/2" sq. (A2b, A3a, B2b, B3a)
- Six 1 3/8" wide strips. From these, cut:
  * 160 – 1 3/8" sq. (A1a, B1a)
- Two 1" wide strips. From these, cut:
  * Eighty – 1" sq. (A1b, B1b)

From Fabric VI, cut: (medium mint green)
- Ten 4 3/8" wide strips. From these, cut:
  * 160 – 2 3/8" x 4 3/8" (A17, B17)

- Ten 1 1/8" wide strips. From these, cut:
  * Eighty – 1 1/8" x 1 3/4" (A10, B10)
  * 240 – 1 1/8" sq. (A7b, A9, B7b, B9)

From Fabric VII, cut: (light mint green)
- Six 3 1/4" wide strips. From these, cut:
  * 160 – 1 3/8" x 3 1/4" (A14, B14)
- Five 2 5/8" wide strips. From these, cut:
  * 160 – 1 1/8" x 2 5/8" (A16a, B16a)
- Six 2 1/4" wide strips. From these, cut:
  * 160 – 1 1/2" x 2 1/4" (A12, B12)
- Eight 1" wide strips. From these, cut:
  * 320 – 1" sq. (A11a, B11a)

Assembly

Making Block A
1. Use diagonal corner technique to make two each of mirror image units 2, 4, 7, and 14. Use this technique to make two of Unit 11. Make one each of units 1, 3, and 6. There are diagonal corners in combined units 11-18. See diagram on page 86 for construction and our instructions below under Block A Assembly.

2. Use diagonal end technique to make two of mirror image Unit 16. Refer to illustration above for correct assembly.

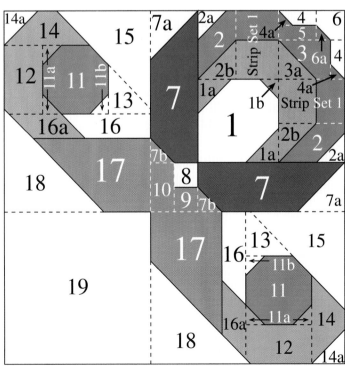

Making mirror image Unit 16 for blocks A & B.

3. The Strip Set diagram at left shows how many strip sets to construct and how many segments to cut from the strip sets. Follow instructions and label the segments in zip top bag.

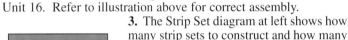

1 1/4" strip

1 1/2" strip

Strip Set 1.
Make 7
Cut into 160 - 1 5/8"

Block A Assembly
1. Refer to block diagram below, and begin by joining units 3 and 4 as shown. Make sure that you have the correct mirror image Unit 4. Join remaining Unit 4 and Unit 5; then add Unit 6 to right side as shown. Join these combined units to combined units

Block A. Make 48. Finishes to 9 1/2" square.

Making combined units 12-15 for Blocks A and B.

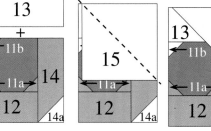

Block B is the border.

2. Refer to the diagram below showing how we assembled the "sets" of Block A so that there would not be a huge bulk to juggle in your embroidery machine if you choose to include the embroideries. For top and bottom, join nine of Block A together as shown. Make four of these "sets." For the center section, we joined six of Block A as illustrated. Make two of these sets. Stitch the embroideries, and join all of the "sets" together.

3-4. Join one mirror image Unit 2 and Strip Set 1. Add to left side of previously joined units to complete top row of flower.

2. Join remaining mirror image Unit 2 with remaining Strip Set 1. Join these combined units to right side of Unit 1 as shown; then add to combined flower top units. Join one mirror image Unit 7 to bottom of flower as shown. Join units 8 and 9; then add Unit 10 to left side of these combined units. Join combined units 8-10 to bottom of remaining mirror image Unit 7; then add to left side of flower.

3. Refer to illustration at top of page. The illustration is shown for the bottom leaf/bud section of Block A. The top leaf/bud on Blocks A and B are mirror images. These combined units are the same for Block B, and you will be referred to them when Block B is assembled. Only the colors change. Begin by joining units 11 and 12; then add Unit 14 to right side of combined units. Join Unit 13 to top as shown; then add diagonal corner Unit 15 as shown. To complete this section, join mirror image Unit 16 and Unit 17; then add to combined 11-15 units. Join Unit 18 as a diagonal corner to other combined units. Join this leaf/bud section to bottom of flower. Make this combined unit section for the top bud, referring frequently to diagram for correct placement of mirror image units.

4. Join Unit 19 to bottom of remaining combined leaf/bud unit; then join them to left side of flower to complete the block. Make 48 of Block A.

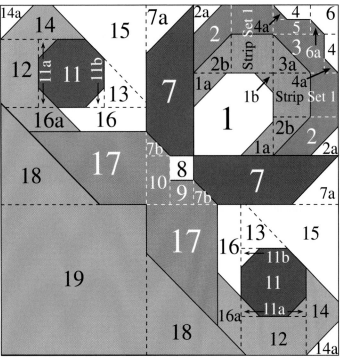

Block B. Make 32 Finishes to 9 1/2" square.

Making Block B

1. Block B is constructed exactly the same as Block A. Refer to all illustrations and assembly instructions for Block A. Make 32 of Block B.

Quilt Assembly

1. In looking at the quilt diagram on page 87, please take note of the fact that Block A comprises the center portion of the quilt, and

joined nine of Block A together as shown. Make four of these "sets." For the center section, we joined six of Block A as illustrated. Make two of these sets. Stitch the embroideries, and join all of the "sets" together.

3. Refer to quilt diagram at right for correct placement of Block B. Join six of Block B in a row as shown. Make two, and join to top and bottom of quilt top, matching seams. Join ten of Block B in a row. Make two and join to opposite sides of quilt top, matching seams.

4. Join previously pieced top and bottom quilt borders; then add remaining borders to opposite sides to complete the quilt top.

QUILTING & FINISHING

All of the patchwork and embroideries were "ditched." For other open areas, a swirl looking motif that had small hearts in the corner areas was used. The dark borders have a feather design that is stitched in a honey brown thread.

We used approximately 360" of straight-grain, French-fold binding to bind the edges.

Finishes to 78" x 95 1/2"

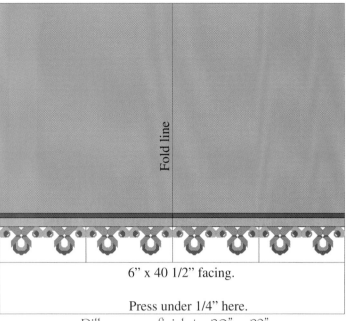

Fold line

6" x 40 1/2" facing.

Press under 1/4" here.

Pillowcases finish to 20" x 29"

Cut completed pillowcase embroideries leaving 1" at top for seam allowance, and 1/4" on sides and bottom.

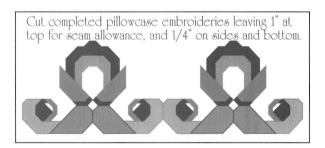

MAKING THE PILLOWCASES

MATERIALS

Fabric I (ivory print)	Need 60"	1 3/4 yards
Fabric II (floral teal and tan print)	Need 48"	1 1/2 yards
Fabric III (dark teal print)	Need 2"	1/8 yard
Fabric IV (light gold linen)	Need 3"	1/8 yard

CUTTING

From Fabric I, cut: (ivory print)
• Four 12" wide strips. From these, cut:
    * Eight – 12" x 20" (for embroideries to fit in mega hoop). When embroideries are complete, cut to 4 1/2" x 10 1/2".
• Two 6" wide strips cut to 40 1/2" long for pillowcase facing.

From Fabric II, cut: (floral teal and tan print)
• Two 24" x 40 1/2" strips for main part of pillowcase.

From Fabric III, cut: (dark teal print)
• Two 1" x 40 1/2" strips for dark border.

From Fabric IV cut: (light gold linen)
• Two 1 1/2" x 40 1/2" strips for border next to embroideries.

Making The Pillowcases
1. Stitch the embroideries, and join four in a row as shown on pillowcase drawing above. Add the 6" wide strip of Fabric I below the embroidered row for the facing. Join the linen strip above the embroideries; then add Fabric III strip. Join the remaining Fabric II piece for the main part of the pillowcase and press.
2. Fold the pillowcase in half, right sides together, and serge or use overcast stitch around 2 sides, leaving bottom open. Turn

right side out and press under 1/4" hem. Press the lining up inside. Turn pillowcase wrong side out, and whip stitch the lining in place. Lining should cover raw seams of border.

MAKING THE DRESSER SCARF

Cut from ivory linen: (we used a medium weight)
• Two – 13 1/2" squares (center squares). To be embroidered.
Cut from light gold linen: (we used medium weight)
• Three– 10 1/8" squares for embroidery. See illustration.

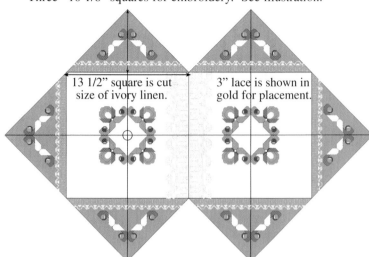

13 1/2" square is cut size of ivory linen.

3" lace is shown in gold for placement.

Please note that diagonal cutting is done after embroideries are complete. See illustration at right.

You will need 2 1/4 yards of 1" wide flat lace and 7/8 yard of 3" wide flat lace.

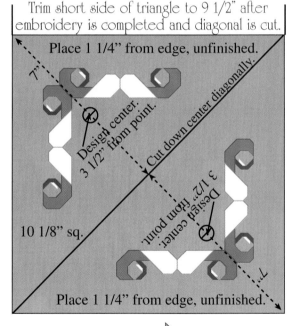

Trim short side of triangle to 9 1/2" after embroidery is completed and diagonal is cut.

Place 1 1/4" from edge, unfinished.

7"

Design center. 3 1/2" from point.

Cut down center diagonally.

Design center. 3 1/2" from point.

10 1/8" sq.

7"

Place 1 1/4" from edge, unfinished.

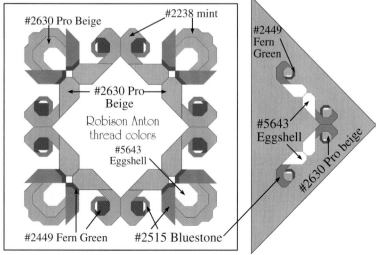

#2630 Pro Beige

#2238 mint

#2630 Pro Beige

Robison Anton thread colors

#5643 Eggshell

#2449 Fern Green

#2515 Bluestone

#2449 Fern Green

#5643 Eggshell

#2630 Pro beige

ASSEMBLY

1. After embroidery completion, place 3" wide flat lace face up along one side of each 13 1/2" ivory embroidered square. Pin in place. Place the 13 1/2" squares right sides together and pin together along side that has lace. Stitch, using 1/4" seam. Press seam open and make sure that lace is lying flat.

2. Pin 1" wide flat lace right side up along long edge of embroidered gold linen triangles. Join long edge of triangles (right sides together) to center section as shown in diagram. Press seams open and trim points.

3. For backing, we used the ivory linen and placed the finished top right side down on the backing. Cut the backing to match the top and pin together securely. Stitch around edge using 1/4" seams and leave at least a 6" opening to turn.

4. Trim at indention and points. Turn right side out and press edges. Slip stitch opening closed.

CUTTING FOR BUFFET CLOTH

☐ **From Fabric I, cut: (muslin)**
- One 6 1/8" wide strip. From this, cut:
  * Two – 6 1/8" sq. (D8b, E8b)
  * Two – 2 1/2" x 6 1/8" (D3, E3)
  * Two – 5" x 8 7/8" (B7, C7)
  * One – 1 5/8" x 5" (A11)
  * Two – 1 1/2" x 5" (B5, C5)
  * Two – 1 1/8" x 5" (B6, C6)
- One 4 3/4" wide strip. From this, cut:
  * Four – 1 1/2" x 4 3/4" (A8, A9)
  * Two – 2 1/4" x 4 5/8" (A4)
  * One – 4 1/2" sq. (D4, E4) Cut in half diagonally to = two triangles.
  * Two – 2 3/8" x 4 3/8" (B3, C3)
  * Two – 7/8" x 4 3/8" (B2, C2)
  * Four – 2 1/2" sq. (B4b, B4c, C4b, C4c)
- One 2 3/4" wide strip. From this, cut:
  * Two – 2 3/4" x 3 5/8" (A19)
  * Two – 2 1/2" x 2 3/4" (D2, E2)
  * Two – 1 5/8" x 2 3/4" (A18)
  * Two – 2" x 2 1/4" (A3)
  * Four – 2 1/8" sq. (A21a, A21b)
  * Four – 2" sq. (A21c, A21d)

- One 1 7/8" wide strip. From this, cut:
  * Four – 1 7/8" sq. (B1b, B1c, C1b, C1c)
  * Twenty-one – 1 5/8" sq. (A6a, A16a, A20a, B1a, C1a, B4a, C4a, D1a, E1a)
- One 1 5/8" wide strip. From this, cut:
  * Fifteen – 1 5/8" sq. (add to 1 5/8" sq. above)
  * Two – 1 3/8" x 1 5/8" (A15)
  * Two – 1 1/4" sq. (A1a)
  * Eight – 1" sq. (A2a, A5a)
- Two 1 1/2" wide strips. From these, cut:
  * Four – 1 1/2" x 4 1/8" (A7)
  * Thirty – 1 1/2" sq. (F5, G5, H5)
- Three 7/8" wide strips. From these, cut:
  * Sixty – 7/8" x 1" (F3, G3, H3)
  * Sixty – 7/8" sq. (F2a, G2a, H2a)

☐ **From Fabric II, cut: (blue and tan floral print)**
- One 9 1/2" wide strip. From this, cut:
  * Two – 9 1/2" sq. (D8a, E8a)
  * Two – 3 7/8" x 8 7/8" (B8, C8)
  * One – 1 5/8" x 5" (A10)
  * Two – 2 3/4" x 3 5/8" (A12)
  * One – 3 1/8" sq. (D5, E5) Cut in half diagonally to = two triangles.
  * Two – 1 5/8" x 2 3/4" (A17)

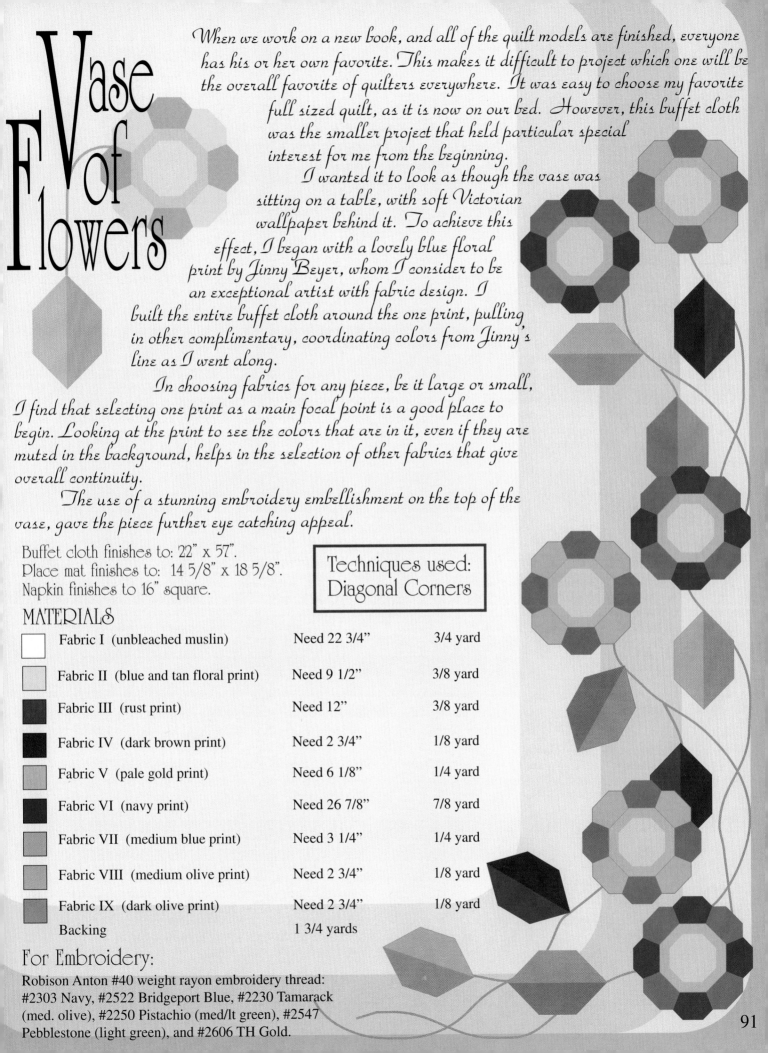

Vase of Flowers

When we work on a new book, and all of the quilt models are finished, everyone has his or her own favorite. This makes it difficult to project which one will be the overall favorite of quilters everywhere. It was easy to choose my favorite full sized quilt, as it is now on our bed. However, this buffet cloth was the smaller project that held particular special interest for me from the beginning.

I wanted it to look as though the vase was sitting on a table, with soft Victorian wallpaper behind it. To achieve this effect, I began with a lovely blue floral print by Jinny Beyer, whom I consider to be an exceptional artist with fabric design. I built the entire buffet cloth around the one print, pulling in other complimentary, coordinating colors from Jinny's line as I went along.

In choosing fabrics for any piece, be it large or small, I find that selecting one print as a main focal point is a good place to begin. Looking at the print to see the colors that are in it, even if they are muted in the background, helps in the selection of other fabrics that give overall continuity.

The use of a stunning embroidery embellishment on the top of the vase, gave the piece further eye catching appeal.

Buffet cloth finishes to: 22" x 57".
Place mat finishes to: 14 5/8" x 18 5/8".
Napkin finishes to 16" square.

> Techniques used:
> Diagonal Corners

MATERIALS

	Fabric I (unbleached muslin)	Need 22 3/4"	3/4 yard
	Fabric II (blue and tan floral print)	Need 9 1/2"	3/8 yard
	Fabric III (rust print)	Need 12"	3/8 yard
	Fabric IV (dark brown print)	Need 2 3/4"	1/8 yard
	Fabric V (pale gold print)	Need 6 1/8"	1/4 yard
	Fabric VI (navy print)	Need 26 7/8"	7/8 yard
	Fabric VII (medium blue print)	Need 3 1/4"	1/4 yard
	Fabric VIII (medium olive print)	Need 2 3/4"	1/8 yard
	Fabric IX (dark olive print)	Need 2 3/4"	1/8 yard
	Backing		1 3/4 yards

For Embroidery:
Robison Anton #40 weight rayon embroidery thread:
#2303 Navy, #2522 Bridgeport Blue, #2230 Tamarack
(med. olive), #2250 Pistachio (med/lt green), #2547
Pebblestone (light green), and #2606 TH Gold.

- From scrap, cut:
  * Two – 1 3/8" x 1 5/8" (A14)
  * Twelve – 1 5/8" sq. (A13a, A16b)
  * Two – 1 1/2" sq. (H5)
  * Four – 7/8" x 1" (H3)
  * Four – 7/8" sq. (H2a)

 From Fabric III, cut: (rust print)
• One 12" x 18" (A5) for embroidery. After embroidery is complete, center it and cut down to a 2" x 10" piece. From scrap, cut:
  * One – 1 5/8" x 5 1/8" (Q1)

 From Fabric IV, cut: (dark brown print)
• One 2 3/4" wide strip. From this, cut:
  * Six – 2 3/4" x 4 1/8" (A13, A20, D1, E1)

 From Fabric V, cut: (pale gold print)
• One 3 1/8" wide strip. From this, cut:
  * One – 3 1/8" x 6 1/2" (A1)
  * Eight – 3" sq. (F1, G1, H1)
  * Two – 1" sq. (Q1a)
• One 1 5/8" wide strip. From this, cut:
  * Two – 1 5/8" x 15 1/2" (Q2)
• One 1 3/8" wide strip. From this, cut:
  * Two – 1 3/8" x 15" (D6, E6)

 From Fabric VI, cut: (navy print)
• One 11 7/8" wide strip. From this, cut:
  * One – 11 7/8" sq. (D8, E8)
  * Two – 1 7/8" x 18" (D7, E7)
  * Sixteen – 1 1/2" x 2" (F2, H2)
  * Sixteen – 1 1/4" sq. (F1a, H1a)
  * Sixteen – 1 1/8" sq. (F5a, H5a)
  * Thirty-two – 1" x 1 1/8" (F4, H4)
  * One – 2" x 3" (A2)
• Six 2 1/2" wide strips. Four for straight-grain binding. From remaining strips, cut:
  * Two – 2 1/2" x 35 1/4" (Q3)

 From Fabric VII, cut: (medium blue print)
• One 2" wide strip. From this, cut:
  * Sixteen – 1 1/2" x 2" (G2)
  * Thirty-two – 1" x 1 1/8" (G4)
• One 1 1/4" wide strip. From this, cut:
  * Sixteen – 1 1/4" sq. (G1a)
  * Sixteen– 1 1/8" sq. (G5a)

 From Fabric VIII, cut: (medium olive print)
• One 2 3/4" wide strip. From this, cut:
  * Four – 2 3/4" x 5" (A21, B4, C4)

From Fabric IX, cut: (dark olive print)
• One 2 3/4" wide strip. From this, cut:
  * Two – 2 3/4" x 4 3/8" (B1, C1)
  * Four – 2 3/4" x 4 1/8" (A6, A16)

Assembly

Making Section A

1. To make Section A, the flowers must be assembled first. The instructions given for diagonal corners apply to all flowers.

2. Use diagonal corner technique to make four each of units 2 and 5. Make one of Unit 1.

3. To assemble the flowers, begin by joining all units 3 and 4. Join combined units 3-4 to opposite sides of Unit 2. Make 4. Join two

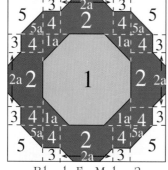

Block F. Make 3
Finishes to: 4 1/2" sq.

of these combined units to top and bottom of Unit 1. Join Unit 5 to opposite short ends of remaining combined 2-4 units; then add to opposite sides of flower.

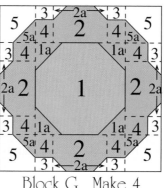

Block G. Make 4
Finishes to: 4 1/2" sq.

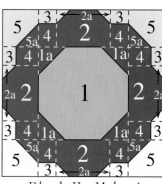

Block H. Make 1
Finishes to: 4 1/2" sq.

4. For Section A, use diagonal corner technique to make two each of units 6, 13, 16, 20, and 21. Make one each of units 1, 2, and 5.

5. To assemble the center section, begin by joining units 3-2-3 in a horizontal row. Join Unit 1 to top of these combined units. Join

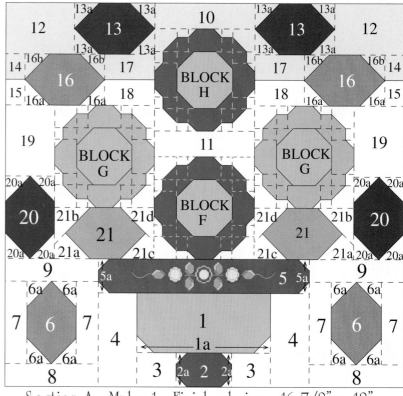

Section A. Make 1. Finished size: 16 7/8" x 18".

Unit 4 to opposite sides of combined units 1-3; then join embroidered Unit 5 to top. For side leaf assembly, join Unit 7 to opposite sides of Unit 6 as shown; then join Unit 8 to bottom and Unit 9 to top. Make two and add them to opposite sides of vase.

6. Refer to diagram above and join Unit 10, Block H, Unit 11, and Block F in a vertical row. Join Unit 21 to bottom of Block G. Join units 19 in 20 as shown; then add the flower/leaf units together. Make 2, referring to diagram for mirror image placement.

7. Join units 17 and 18. Join units 14 and 15. Make a row of combined units 14-15, Unit 16 and combined units 17-18. Join units 12 and 13; then add them to top of combined units 14-18. Make two mirror image, and add them to top of combined units 19-21.

8. Join the flower Block G combined unit sections to opposite sides of center Block F row. Join the top floral section to the bottom vase section to complete Section A.

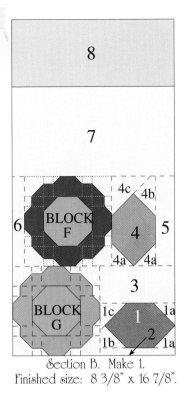

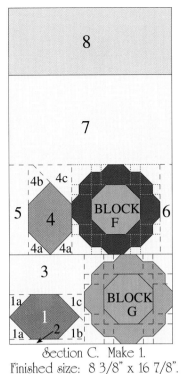

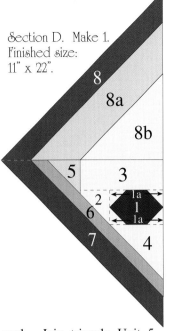

Section D. Make 1.
Finished size: 11" x 22".

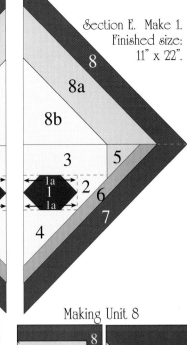

Section E. Make 1.
Finished size: 11" x 22".

Section B. Make 1.
Finished size: 8 3/8" x 16 7/8".

Section C. Make 1.
Finished size: 8 3/8" x 16 7/8".

Making Sections B and C

1. Sections B and C are mirror images. Refer to instructions for making the flower blocks. Make two each of Block F and Block G. For both sections, use diagonal corner technique to make two each of units 1 and 4.

2. To assemble the sections, refer to illustration above frequently for correct placement of mirror image units. Join units 3, 1, and 2 in a vertical row; then add Block G to side of combined units as shown. Join units 5, 4, Block F, and Unit 6 in a row as shown; then add them to top of combined units 1-Block G. Join units 7 and 8; then add them to top of flowers to complete sections B and C.

Making Sections D and E

1. To make top of sections D and E, refer to diagram at right for Making Unit 8. Join diagonal corner 8a to Unit 8 as shown. Join on both sides. Stitch diagonal, trim and press. Join diagonal corner 8b on both sides as shown. Trim and press. Cut square in half diagonally.

2. For bottom of the two sections, refer to diagrams as the following units are mirror images. Join units 1 and 2; then add Unit 3 to top of combined units, and triangle Unit 4 to bottom. Using triangle Unit 4 as a guide, trim off bottom of Unit 2 to match the diagonal. Join triangle Unit 5. Join Unit 6 strip, and trim diagonals. Join Unit 7, and trim diagonals.

3. Join Unit 8 top to combined bottom units to complete sections D and E.

Assembly of Buffet Cloth

1. Refer to diagram below, and join sections A, B, and C together as shown, matching seams.

2. Join Unit Q2 to opposite sides of Unit Q1; then add to bottom of buffet cloth. Join Unit 3 to top and bottom; then join sections D and E as shown.

3. Use 1/4" wide dark green press on bias for the stems, or make your own as described on page 30.

Quilting and Finishing

1. All of the patchwork was "ditched" and the background stippled with a medium stipple stitch.

2. We used approx. 168" of straight-grain, French fold binding to bind the edges.

Making Unit 8

Step 1

Step 2

Step 3

Step 4

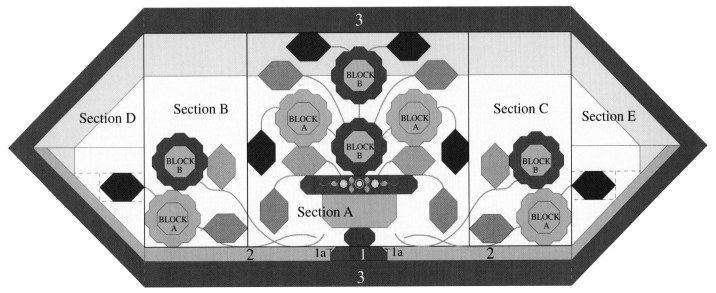

MATERIALS FOR PLACE MATS

☐	Fabric I (unbleached muslin)	Need 35 3/4"	1 1/8 yards
■	Fabric II (rust print)	Need 13 1/4"	1/2 yard
■	Fabric III (dark brown print)	Need 6"	Scrap
☐	Fabric IV (pale gold print)	Need 4 7/8"	1/4 yard
■	Fabric V (navy print)	Need 21 1/4"	3/4 yard
☐	Fabric VI (medium blue print)	Need 3 1/4"	1/4 yard
☐	Fabric VII (medium olive print)	Need 6" sq.	Scrap
☐	Fabric VIII (dark olive print)	Need 6" sq.	Scrap
	Backing for two place mats		1/2 yard

CUTTING FOR TWO PLACE MATS & NAPKINS

☐ **From Fabric I, cut: (muslin)**
- One 20" wide strip. From this, cut:
  * Two – 20" sq. (embroidered napkins) Cut down to 16" square upon completion of embroidery.

* Two – 1 7/8" x 9 1/2" (Q11)
- One 7 1/2" wide strip. From this, cut:
  * Two – 7 1/2" x 15 1/4" (Q12) This unit will be cut down after place mat is embroidered. See illustration.
  * Two – 4 3/4" x 5 3/4" (Q10)
- One 5 " wide strip. From this, cut:
  * Two – 1 7/8" x 5" (Q14)
  * Two – 1 1/4" x 5" (Q15)
  * Two – 1 1/8" x 5" (Q2)
  * Two – 7/8" x 5" (Q3)
  * Do not cut strip width down after 5" cuts as square units will be stacked.
  * Two – 2 3/8" x 4 3/8" (Q4)
  * Two – 7/8" x 4 3/8" (Q6)
  * Two – 1 1/8" x 4 1/4" (Q9)
  * Two – 2" x 4 1/8" (Q8)
  * Four – 2 1/2" sq. (Q1b, Q1c)
  * Four – 1 7/8" sq. (Q5b, Q5c)
  * Sixteen – 1 5/8" sq. (Q1a, Q5a, Q7a)
- One 1 1/2" wide strip. From this, cut:
  * Sixteen – 1 1/2" sq. (F5, G5)
- Two 7/8" wide strips. From these, cut:
  * Thirty-two – 7/8" x 1" (F3, G3)
  * Thirty-two – 7/8" sq. (F2a, G2a)

From Fabric II, cut: (rust print)
- One 8 1/4" wide strip. From this, cut:
  * Two - 8 1/4" x 16 1/2" (Q13) This unit will be cut down after place mat is embroidered. See illustration.
- One 5" wide strip. From this, cut:
  * Two – 5" x 13 1/2" (napkin rings)

From Fabric III, cut: (dark brown print)
- Two – 2 3/4" x 4 1/8" (Q7)

From Fabric IV, cut: (pale gold print)
- One 3" wide strip. From this, cut:
  * Four – 3" sq. (F1, G1)
- One 1 7/8" wide strip. From this, cut:
  * Two – 1 7/8" x 19 18" (Q16)

From Fabric V, cut: (navy print)
- Four 2 1/2" wide strips for straight-grain binding (place mats)
- Five 2" wide strips. Four for straight-grain binding (napkins).

From remaining strip, cut:
  * Eight – 1 1/2" x 2" (F2)
  * Sixteen – 1" x 1 1/8" (F4)
- One 1 1/4" wide strip. From this, cut:
  * Eight – 1 1/4" sq. (F1a)
  * Eight – 1 1/8" sq. (F5a)

From Fabric VI, cut: (medium blue print)
- One 2" wide strip. From this, cut:
  * Eight – 1 1/2" x 2" (G2)
  * Sixteen – 1" x 1 1/8" (G4)
- One 1 1/4" wide strip. From this, cut:
  * Eight – 1 1/4" sq. (G1a)
  * Eight – 1 1/8" sq. (G5a)

From Fabric VII, cut: (medium olive print)
- Two - 2 3/4" x 5" (Q1)

From Fabric VIII, cut: (dark olive print)
- Two – 2 3/4" x 4 3/8" (Q5)

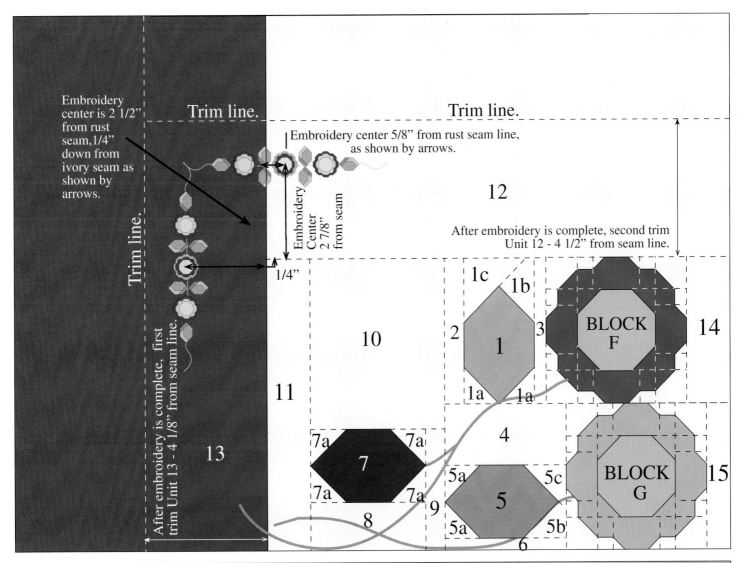

Embroidery center is 2 1/2" from rust seam,1/4" down from ivory seam as shown by arrows.

Trim line.

Trim line.

Embroidery center 5/8" from rust seam line, as shown by arrows.

Trim line.

Embroidery Center 2 7/8" from seam

After embroidery is complete, first trim Unit 13 - 4 1/8" from seam line.

1/4"

12

After embroidery is complete, second trim Unit 12 - 4 1/2" from seam line.

10

11

13

1c 1b
2 1 3
1a 1a

7a 7a
7 7
7a 7a

4

9 5a 5c
5 5
8 5a 5b
6

BLOCK F

14

BLOCK G

15

Add Unit 16 after embroideries are complete and units 12 and 13 are trimmed.

16

Place mat finishes to 14 5/8" x 18 5/8"

Assembly

Assembling The Place mat.

1. Refer to page 92 for instructions on assembling blocks F and G. Make one of each block for each place mat.

2. Use diagonal corner technique to make one each of units 1, 5, and 7. To assemble the place mat, join units 2, 1, 3, Block F, and Unit 14 in a horizontal row as shown. Join units 4, 5 and 6. Join Block G and Unit 15. Join these units together to form another horizontal row. Join the two rows together as shown.

3. Join units 7 and 8; then add Unit 9 to right side of these combined units. Join Unit 10 to top; then add Unit 11 to left side. Join these combined units to flowers; then add Unit 12 to top. Join Unit 13 to left side.

4. Refer to illustration at right for embroidery placement, and stitch the embroideries. The place mat is elegant with the embroideries, however it can be made without them and stand out on any table.

5. Trim units 12 and 13 after embroidery is complete. Join Unit 16 to bottom of place mat.

Napkins

1. Embroidered napkin illustrations show the measurements that we used and suggested fabric colors for the design. We used French-fold binding on both the place mats and napkins.

Napkins are made by embroidering the design on the napkin as shown. 16" squares were cut from two different fabrics for the reversible napkin. Upon completion of the embroidery, place the two 16" squares for the napkin wrong sides together and bind with French-fold binding. This takes a while to do, but we love the results. The napkin folds make convenient pockets in which to place the silverware.

2. To make the napkin rings, fold the 5" x 13 1/2" pieces of Fabric II in half lengthwise, right sides together. Stitch around the raw edges, leaving a small opening to turn. Turn right side out and slip stitch the opening closed. Hand stitch the ends together to fit the napkin after it is folded.

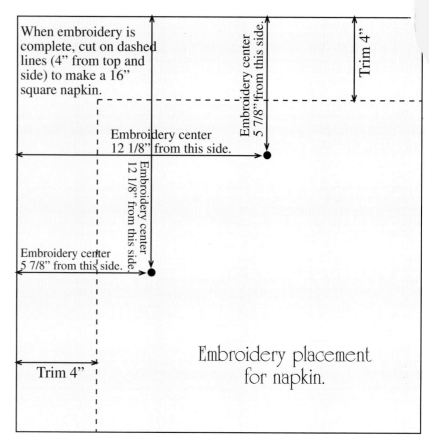

When embroidery is complete, cut on dashed lines (4" from top and side) to make a 16" square napkin.

Trim 4"

Embroidery center 5 7/8" from this side.

Embroidery center 12 1/8" from this side.

Embroidery center 12 1/8" from this side.

Embroidery center 5 7/8" from this side.

Trim 4"

Embroidery placement for napkin.

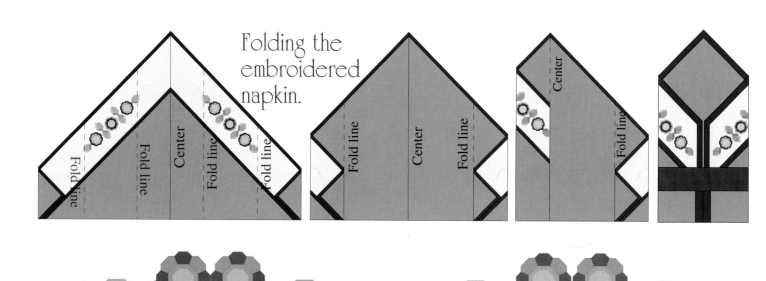

Folding the embroidered napkin.

Baltimore Embroidered Throw

The "Baltimore Throw" embroideries are probably the most significant in our entire collection as they can be used in so many places, and in so many ways.

They are perfect as a whole, or with design elements broken apart for clothing, accomplished easily by using Stitch Editor Plus.

Cutting instructions, and yardages for the entire throw are given in this section.

We hope that you will let your imagination go wild and use the collection for your complete enjoyment.

Finished size: 26 3/4" x 32 3/4"
Blocks finish to 6" square.

Our linen for the throw came from "The Linen House" in Brussels, Belgium. It is 56" wide. We used two colors from their Misto Lino line; Champagne (ivory) and Honey (medium gold). The quality is superb and delivery was excellent. You can access their web site at: http://www.TheLinenHouse.com

We used ivory linen for the backing. Backing measurement will be given separately.

Cutting from 56" wide linen.

From Ivory Linen, cut:
- Four 12" wide strips. From these, cut:
  * Twelve - 12" x 16" for throw block embroideries. After embroideries are complete, center and cut down to 6 1/2" squares.
  * Sixteen - 1 1/4" x 6 1/2" (Q1)
- Six 9" wide strips. From these, cut:
  * Thirty-two - 9" squares for border embroidered flowers. After border flowers are stitched, center ande cut down to 1 7/8" x 3 1/2".
- One 1 1/2" wide strip. From this, cut:
  * Two - 1 1/2" x 21 1/2" (Q3)
- Two 1 1/4" wide strips. From these, cut:
  * Three - 1 1/4" x 21 1/2" (Q2)
- One 1 1/8" wide strip. From this, cut:
  * Two - 1 1/8" x 27 1/2" (Q6)

For top you will need exactly 107 1/8" - 3 1/8 yards.
If used for backing, you will need to cut: 27 1/4" x 33 1/4". You will need 7/8 yard for the backing.

From Medium Gold Linen, cut:
- One 9" wide strip. From this, cut:
  * Four - 9" sq. (Q9) for embroidered throw corners.
- One 8" wide strip. From this, cut:
  * Two - 8" x 26 3/4" (fringe - DO NOT FRINGE until throw is completed)
- Two 1 3/8" wide strips. From these, cut:
  * Two - 1 3/8" x 27 1/2" (Q8)
  * Two - 1 3/8" x 21 1/2" (Q5)

You will need 19 3/4" - 5/8 yard.

Assembly

1. Refer to throw illustration for correct placement of blocks. Make four rows of blocks, beginning and ending with a Q1 sashing strip. Join rows with Q2 sashing strips between them and Q3 sashing strips at top and bottom.

2. Make two rows of seven embroidered border flowers and join them to top and bottom of throw. Pin securely when joining the flowers, so that leaf tips match. Join Unit Q5 to top and bottom of throw.

3. Make two rows of nine embroidered border flowers and join sashing strip Q6 to bottom of floral row, and Q8 to the top as shown in illustration. Refer to diagram for correct placement of corner flowers, and join corner flowers to opposite short ends of the floral border rows. Join to opposite sides of throw, again matching leaf tips to complete throw top.

4. To assemble throw with gold linen for fringe, place the two fringe pieces right sides facing at top and bottom of throw, with raw edges matching. The fringe will be 1/4" away from side raw edges so that it is not sewn into side seams.

5. Place backing right sides facing on throw front and pin securely. Stitch around outside edge of throw through all thicknesses. Leave about a 6-8" opening to turn. Turn right side out and press from the back side. Fray the fringe to the edge of the throw.

Robison Anton thread colors.

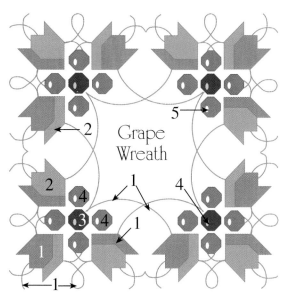

Grape Wreath

#1 - Desert cactus, #2544 - #2 - Pistacio, #2250
#3 - Intense maroon, #2587 - #4 - Satin wine, #2314 - #5 - Ivory, 2335

Fleur-de-Lis

#1 - Hazel, #2481 -#2 - Lt. bronze, #2493 -#3 -Bridgeport blue, #2522
#4 - Slate blue, #2275 - 5 - Salem blue - #2534 -#6 -TH Gold, #2606
#7 - Lt. bronze, #2493 -#8 - Pistacio, #2250 -#9 - Desert cactus, #2544

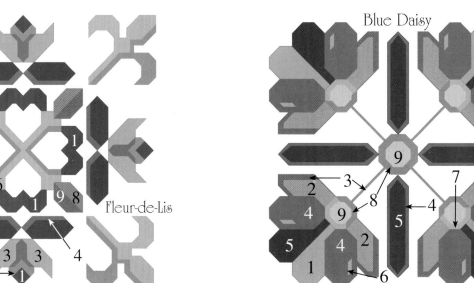

Blue Daisy

#1 & 6 - Bridgeport blue, #2522 - #2 - Pistacio, #2250
#3 - Desert cactus, #2544 - #4 - Slate blue, #2275 -#5 - Salem blue, #2534
#7 - TH gold, #2606 -#8 - Lt. bronze, #2493 - #9 - Pro maize, #2732

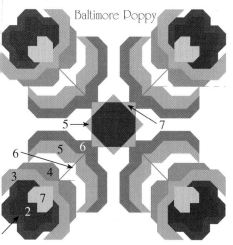

Baltimore Poppy

#1 - Red berry, #2418 - #2 - Russet, #2252
#3 & 5 - Nile - #2211 - #4 - Pistacio - #2250
#6 - Desert cactus, #2544
#7 - TH gold - 2606

Hearts & Flowers

#1 - Bridgeport blue, #2522 - #2 - Lt. bronze, #2493
#3 - TH gold, #2606 - #4 & 9 - Salem blue - #2534
#5 - Terra cotta, #2334 - #6 - TH gold, #2606
#7 - Desert cactus, #2544 - #8, Pistacio - #2250

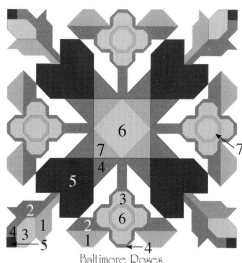

Baltimore Roses

#1 - Pistacio, #2250 - #2 - Desert castus, #2544
#3 - Pink, #2223 - #4 - Rose tint, #2591
#5 - Russet, #2252 - #6 - Pro maize, #2732
#7 - TH gold, #2606

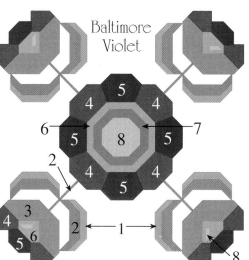

Baltimore Violet

#1 - Pebblestone, #2547 - #2 - Nile, #2211
#3 - Lavender, #2276 - #4 - Cachet, #2424
#5 - Laurie lilac, #2425 - #6 - TH gold, #2606
#7 - Light bronze, #2493 - #8 - Pro maize, #2732

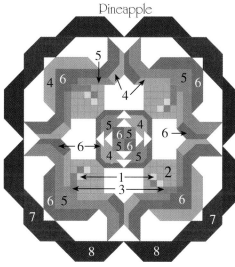

Pineapple

#1 - Pro maize, #2732 - #2 - TH gold, #2606
#3 - Ashley gold, #2401 - #4 - Pistacio, #2250
#5 - Tamarack - #2230 - #6 - Desert cactus, #2544
#7 - Red berry, #2418 - #8 - Russet, #2252

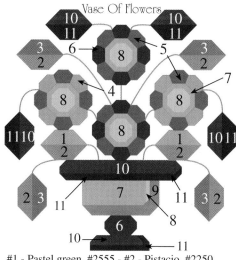

Vase Of Flowers

#1 - Pastel green, #2555 - #2 - Pistacio, #2250
#3 - Desert cactus, #2544 - #4 - Ice blue, #2300
#5 - Rockport blue, #2536 - #6 - Salem blue, #2534
#7 - TH gold, #2606 - #8 - Pro maize, #2732
#9 - Lt. Bronze, #2493 - #10 - Rust, #2289
#11 - Terra cotta, #2334

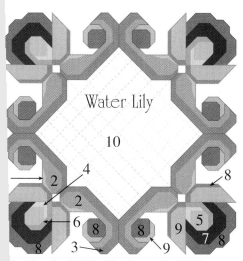

Water Lily

1 - Pistacio, #2250 - #2 - Tamarack, #2230
3 - Desert cactus, #2544 - #4 - Pro maize, #2732
5 - TH gold, #2606 - #6 & 10 - Lt. bronze - #2493
7 - Maroon, #2587 - #8 - Satin wine, #2314
9 - Lavender, #2276

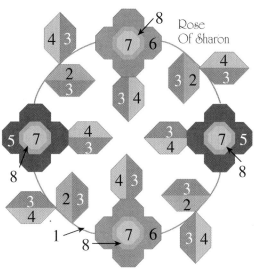

Rose Of Sharon

#1 - Desert cactus, #2544 - #2 - Pastel green, #2550
#3 - Green dust, #2457 - #4 - Pistacio, #2250
#5 - Laurie lilac, #2425 - #6 - Cachet, #2424
#7 - Pro maize, #2732 - #8 - TH gold, #2606

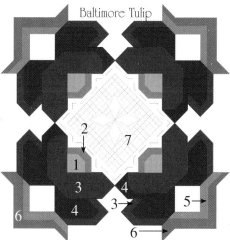

Baltimore Tulip

#1 - TH gold, #2606 - #2 & 7 - Lt. bronze - #2493
#3 - Red berry - #2418 - #4 - Russet - #2252
#5 - Nile - #2211 - #6 - Pro Erin - #2738

Border Flower

#1 - Pistacio, #2250
#2 - Desert Cactus, #2544
#3 - Russet, #2252
#4 - TH Gold, #2606
#5 - Pro beige, #2630

Corner Flower

Other Books By Pam Bono Designs, Inc.

Quick Rotary Cutter Quilts - Oxmoor House/Leisure Arts

More Quick Rotary Cutter Quilts - Oxmoor House/Leisure Arts.

Quilt It For Kids - C & T Publishing

A Quilter's Life In Patchwork book and CD-ROM - Pam Bono Designs, Inc.,. and June Tailor, Inc.

Look for these fine books and patterns by Pam Bono Designs in your local quilt or fabric shop.

"The Angler 2™" may be purchased where ever notions are sold.

Web site:
http://www.pambonodesigns.com

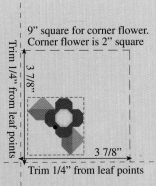

9" square for corner flower.
Corner flower is 2" square

3 7/8"

Trim 1/4" from leaf points

3 7/8"

Trim 1/4" from leaf points

Cutting for corner flower